HEALTH INSURANCE

ISSUES, CHALLENGES AND PERSPECTIVES

Health Care Issues, Costs and Access

Additional books in this series can be found on Nova's website
under the Series tab.

Additional E-books in this series can be found on Nova's website
under the E-books tab.

Public Health in the 21st Century

Additional books in this series can be found on Nova's website
under the Series tab.

Additional E-books in this series can be found on Nova's website
under the E-books tab.

HEALTH INSURANCE

ISSUES, CHALLENGES AND PERSPECTIVES

EDVARD ABRAHAMSEN

AND

AASTA FAGERLAND

EDITORS

Nova Science Publishers, Inc.

New York

Copyright © 2012 by Nova Science Publishers, Inc.

All rights reserved. No part of this book may be reproduced, stored in a retrieval system or transmitted in any form or by any means: electronic, electrostatic, magnetic, tape, mechanical photocopying, recording or otherwise without the written permission of the Publisher.

For permission to use material from this book please contact us:
Telephone 631-231-7269; Fax 631-231-8175
Web Site: http://www.novapublishers.com

NOTICE TO THE READER

The Publisher has taken reasonable care in the preparation of this book, but makes no expressed or implied warranty of any kind and assumes no responsibility for any errors or omissions. No liability is assumed for incidental or consequential damages in connection with or arising out of information contained in this book. The Publisher shall not be liable for any special, consequential, or exemplary damages resulting, in whole or in part, from the readers' use of, or reliance upon, this material. Any parts of this book based on government reports are so indicated and copyright is claimed for those parts to the extent applicable to compilations of such works.

Independent verification should be sought for any data, advice or recommendations contained in this book. In addition, no responsibility is assumed by the publisher for any injury and/or damage to persons or property arising from any methods, products, instructions, ideas or otherwise contained in this publication.

This publication is designed to provide accurate and authoritative information with regard to the subject matter covered herein. It is sold with the clear understanding that the Publisher is not engaged in rendering legal or any other professional services. If legal or any other expert assistance is required, the services of a competent person should be sought. FROM A DECLARATION OF PARTICIPANTS JOINTLY ADOPTED BY A COMMITTEE OF THE AMERICAN BAR ASSOCIATION AND A COMMITTEE OF PUBLISHERS.

Additional color graphics may be available in the e-book version of this book.

LIBRARY OF CONGRESS CATALOGING-IN-PUBLICATION DATA

ISBN: 978-1-62081-050-7

Published by Nova Science Publishers, Inc. † New York

CONTENTS

PREFACE

In this book, the authors present current research in the study of the issues and challenges of health care insurance from across the globe. Topics discussed in this compilation include the assessment of the efficiency of hospitals in Botswana; the public long-term care insurance system in Japan; an examination of service delivery when there is an integration of health insurance and care provisions; estimating the total health expenditure on households by sources of financing and providers in Gambia; and social and private insurance systems in The Netherlands.

Chapter 1 - The objective of this study was to estimate the total health expenditure by sources of financing, financing agents and providers. The study followed the standard methods spelt out in the WHO guide to producing national health accounts (NHA). The information on household expenditure on health was obtained from the Integrated Household Survey (IHS) and a small scale household survey conducted in 2006 on health seeking behaviour. Household health expenditure data was obtained from scientifically drawn samples of 4800 households in the 2003 Integrated Household Survey and 1000 households in the Household Health Expenditure and Utilization Survey (HHEUS) conducted in 2006. Organizational survey data was obtained from 41 public health care providers, 18 private/NGO health care providers, 5 government departments, 7 local government areas, 14 donors, 20 NGOs, 1 insurance company, and 70 employer/private firms. The data was extracted from the questionnaires, entered and analysed in Excel spreadsheet. The total health expenditure (THE) was approximately Dalasi (GMD) 1,185,223,103 in 2002; GMD 1,395,958,522 in 2003; and GMD 1,682,323,673 in 2004. THE as a percentage of Gross Domestic Product (GDP) in The Gambia was 16.1% in 2002, 13.9% in 2003 and 14.9% in 2004. The per capita total health expenditure was GMD 895 (US\$23.5) in 2002, GMD 1026 (US\$26.9) in 2003 and GMD 1203 (US\$31.6) in 2004. During the three years over 66% of the total health funding came from donors (international health development partners). The Government of The Gambia contribution grew from 18% in 2002 to 24% of the total health expenditure in 2004. The households, through direct out-of-pocket payments to health care providers, contributed 12% in 2002, 11% in 2003 and 9% in 2004 to the total health expenditure. The NHA evidence will inform health decision-making, including policy and plan development. In addition, the results of the study will help government identify better policy instruments to re-orient the way health- finances are to be distributed in The Gambia, and will hopefully enable policy makers to better understand the flow of resources in the health system. Furthermore, the results could be used to negotiate with multilateral and bilateral agencies for additional funding for the health sector.

Chapter 2 - The Netherlands has a long tradition of health insurance based on the combination of both social and private insurance systems respectively. On January 1 2006 a new Health Insurance Act (Zorgverzekeringswet) (HIA), came into force. Under this Act all residents of the Netherlands are legally obliged to take out a basic health insurance which covers standard medical expenses such as General Practitioner, hospitals costs or pharmaceutical costs. As in many countries, vulnerable groups such as the homeless and those addicted to drugs and alcohol, are often uninsured for the cost of medical care. With the advent of the new HIA, it was anticipated that higher premium contributions, own risk levels and administrative procedures would lead to an increase in the number of people without adequate health insurance. A lack of health insurance has serious consequences, not only for the individuals concerned, but also for the accessibility, utilisation and quality of healthcare. In the city of Utrecht, several provisions have been put in place to improve the level of insurance of vulnerable groups and those affected by the Health Insurance Act and to maintain their insurance. In order to evaluate these provisions, the health insurance status of a group of 3,168 Public Mental Health care (PMHc) clients in the city of Utrecht was followed from July 2004 to January 2008, both retrospectively and prospectively. The percentage of uninsured PMHc clients showed a decrease from 27.4% in July 2004 to 12.4% in January 2008. The decrease was most noticeable in the group of addicted persons. However, the decline stagnated in the course of 2008. It was recommended to intensify case management in order to further decrease the proportion of uninsured in this client group. Of the original 2004 cohort, 245 persons had died, 33 had left the country and 178 were not found in any health insurance register. For the remaining cohort members a trend analysis was made. In January 2011 12.0% of the cohort members were uninsured, with higher percentages among persons younger than 40 (15.3%) and non-Dutch clients (13.9%) and a lower percentage among clients with a personal case manager (13.5%). Since case management seems to reduce the proportion of uninsured subjects the recommendation is to continue to focus on and intensify case management across all vulnerable groups.

Chapter 3 - The health system in sub-Saharan Africa faces a number of challenges, including weak health systems structures. The ramifications of inefficiencies in the management of resources could jeopardise the development of health infrastructure and the coverage of health care, especially among the poor and underprevillaged. Consequently, efficient allocation and management of scarce resources could improve the health systems in the region. The 2010 World Health Report places much emphasis on the invaluable role that efficiency palys in achieving universal coverage. The aim of this chapter was to conduct an exploratory assessment of the performance of non-referral hospitals in Botswana for the period 2006 to 2008 using the Pabón Lasso technique. The results show that during each year in the study period, less than half of the hospitals operated efficiently while more than half operated with excess bed capacity. The findings of the study imply that rather than expanding hospital sizes by increasing the number of beds, there could be an expansion in the health services provided by hospitals. This provides an opportunity to improve maternal and child health services and accelerate progress towards the health-related Millennium Development Goal targets while moving the country towards universal coverage of health services.

Chapter 4 - Improvements in public health and advances in medicine after World War II have given Japan one of the highest life expectancies in the world. The dramatic increase in the number of older people in this country is well documented. Because the birth rate dropped sharply after the postwar baby boom, population aging is proceeding more rapidly than in any other industrialized nation. Due to the increased population, the number of elderly in need of care has also increased. It is estimated that the number of elderly in need of care will reach 5.2 million in 2020. Therefore, in April 2000, a new public long-term care insurance system (LTCIS) was launched in Japan, making it the third country to do so, after the Netherlands and Germany. Although Japanese LTCIS follows the German LTCIS, there are some differences between the two countries. First, the elderly in need of care and their caregivers choose to receive care services or cash payment for family-based caregiving in German, while only care services are available in Japan. Second, caremanager, who arranged care services as well as assess the effect of care services, help users to make a care plan in Japan, although the idea of care management was adopted from the United Kingdoms' system. In this chapter, the authors introduce Japanese LTCIS and the authors studies on the care burden among caregivers before and after the introduction of this system.

Chapter 5 - What happens to the delivery of health services when health insurers integrate with care providers? Health insurers and care providers can choose among different methods when organizing their mutual transactions. The authors distinguish between standard market- and hierarchical organization. In hierarchies, health insurance and care provision are integrated and coordinated by an overarching entity. This entity may want to lower costs in order to increase its profits. While this behavior may be desirable in light of the growing costs of health care, consumers and policy-makers fear that this containment of costs will come at the expense of quality. The authors test both hypotheses by analyzing empirical literature and find a strong negative link between integration and costs. Regarding quality, evidence is mixed. Integration seems to alter care experiences, reflecting skepticism towards or discomfort with the entity's dominant role in providing health care. Objective quality data, such as mortality rates, fail to show a consistent negative effect of integration on health. Regarding the effect of integration on care processes, hierarchies excel in the provision of preventive care, but underprovide services to those who are most in need of health care. The authors explain the authors findings by referring to incentive structures at both the organizational and physician level. The authors conclude that integration of health insurance and care provision may only be beneficial for subgroups of patients. This implies that, optimally, governments should create a legal base for hierarchical organization while initiating quality transparency, such that these subgroups can select themselves into hierarchies.

In: Health Insurance
Editors: E. Abrahamsen et al.

ISBN: 978-1-62081-050-7
© 2012 Nova Science Publishers, Inc.

Chapter 1

REPUBLIC OF THE GAMBIA NATIONAL HEALTH ACCOUNTS: 2002-2004

Sekou Omar Touray[1,], Joses Muthuri Kirigia[2,†],
Eyob Zere[2], Momodou K. Cham[3], Ceesay Momodou[4],
J. Bukhari Sillah[5] and Mamat Cham[1]*

[1]Department of State for Health and Social Welfare,
Banjul, the Gambia
[2]World Health Organization, Regional Office for Africa,
Brazzaville, Congo
[3]National Planning Commission, Banjul, the Gambia
[4]WHO Country Office, Banjul, the Gambia
[5]Department of Economics, University of The Gambia,
Banjul, the Gambia

ABSTRACT

The objective of this study was to estimate the total health expenditure by sources of financing, financing agents and providers. The study followed the standard methods spelt out in the WHO guide to producing national health accounts (NHA). The information on

[*] E-mail: sekougam@hotmail.com.
[†] E-mail: kirigiaj@afro.who.int Tel: +4724139342.

household expenditure on health was obtained from the Integrated Household Survey (IHS) and a small scale household survey conducted in 2006 on health seeking behaviour.

Household health expenditure data was obtained from scientifically drawn samples of 4800 households in the 2003 Integrated Household Survey and 1000 households in the Household Health Expenditure and Utilization Survey (HHEUS) conducted in 2006. Organizational survey data was obtained from 41 public health care providers, 18 private/NGO health care providers, 5 government departments, 7 local government areas, 14 donors, 20 NGOs, 1 insurance company, and 70 employer/private firms. The data was extracted from the questionnaires, entered and analysed in Excel spreadsheet.

The total health expenditure (THE) was approximately Dalasi (GMD) 1,185,223,103 in 2002; GMD 1,395,958,522 in 2003; and GMD 1,682,323,673 in 2004. THE as a percentage of Gross Domestic Product (GDP) in The Gambia was 16.1% in 2002, 13.9% in 2003 and 14.9% in 2004. The per capita total health expenditure was GMD 895 (US$23.5) in 2002, GMD 1026 (US$26.9) in 2003 and GMD 1203 (US$31.6) in 2004. During the three years over 66% of the total health funding came from donors (international health development partners). The Government of The Gambia contribution grew from 18% in 2002 to 24% of the total health expenditure in 2004. The households, through direct out-of-pocket payments to health care providers, contributed 12% in 2002, 11% in 2003 and 9% in 2004 to the total health expenditure.

The NHA evidence will inform health decision-making, including policy and plan development. In addition, the results of the study will help government identify better policy instruments to re-orient the way health- finances are to be distributed in The Gambia, and will hopefully enable policy makers to better understand the flow of resources in the health system. Furthermore, the results could be used to negotiate with multilateral and bilateral agencies for additional funding for the health sector.

Keywords: The Gambia, national health accounts, total health expenditure, out-of-pocket payments.

1. INTRODUCTION

The Gambia is located on the West African coast. It is bordered on the North, South and East by the Republic of Senegal and on the West by the

Atlantic Ocean. The country has a surface land area of 10,689 square kilometres. The country has a tropical climate characterised by 2 seasons, rainy season June-October and dry season November-May.

In 2004 the population of Gambia was estimated at 1.478 million and growing 3.2% per year. About 60% of the population live in the rural areas. The country has a total fertility rate of 4.6 and a dependency ratio of 79 per 100 (WHO 2006).

The Gambia has 4 public referral hospitals, 6 public district hospitals (or Major Health Centres), 31 minor public health centres, 8 private/NGO hospitals and 11 private/NGO health centres DOHSW (Government of the Gambia 2006). The services of the fixed health facilities are augmented by Village Health Workers and Traditional Birth Attendants.

The national health system is manned by 156 (i.e. 0.11 per 1000 population) physicians, 1719 (1.21 per 1000 population) nurses, 162 midwives (0.11 per 1000 population), 43 (0.03 per 1000 population) dentists, 48 (0.03 per 1000 population) pharmacists, 33 (0.02 per 1000 population) public and environmental health workers, 968 community health workers (0.68 per 1000 population), 99 (0.07 per 1000 population) laboratory technicians, 3 (0.00 per 1000 population) other health workers, and 391 (0.27 per 1000 population) health management and support workers were in the Republic of Gambia (WHO 2006).

The 2004 life expectancy of Gambia (57 years) was equal to that of Ghana. It was the second highest among the Economic Community of West African States (ECOWAS) after that of Cape Verde (70 years). The life expectancy in Gambia was 7 years higher than the average for ECOWAS, which was 50 years. In Gambia, the life expectancy for males was 55 years and female was 59 years (WHO 2006).

The under-5 mortality rate (for both sexes) in Gambia was 122 per 1000, which was second lowest in ECOWAS, after Cape Verde. The Gambia under-five mortality rate for males (129 per 1000) was higher than that of females (115 per 1000). The under-5 mortality rate in Gambia was lower than the average for ECOWAS of 178 per 1000 (male=183/1000 and female=168/1000) (WHO 2006).

The adult mortality rate for Gambia was 304 per 1000, which was lower than that of all the other ECOWAS countries, except for Cape Verde. The average adult mortality rate for ECOWAS was 410 per 1000 and the median was 441 per 1000. The Gambia adult male mortality rate was 344 per 1000 and that for females was 263 per 1000 (WHO 2006).

The Government has been implementing various health sector reforms geared at improving the health indicators mentioned above (Government of the Gambia 1980, 1988, 2000, 2002). In 2002 the Gambian Department of Health and Social Welfare (DOSH) decided to undertake the first National Health Accounts (NHA) study to establish the total health financing in Gambia with a view to garnering evidence that would inform the implementation of the health sector reforms stipulated in her national health policy and strategic health development plan.

The specific objectives of the study were to: trace the sources of health expenditure in Gambia; determine total health expenditure by financing agents and providers; examine the distribution of funds by functions e.g. prevention and curative services; and trace the channels of distribution of funds by inputs (line items), e.g. personnel remunerations, medicines.

2. METHODS

2.1. NHA Conceptual Framework

National Health Accounts was designed to provide a comprehensive description of the flow of resources from the source to the ultimate use. This is the first time that the NHA tool (WHO 2003) has been used by the DOHSW in The Gambia. International experience in the development and use of health accounts suggests a number of useful dimensions (WHO 2003):

a) *Financing sources:* Institutions or entities that provide funds used in the health system by financing agents. The financing sources in The Gambia consist of the Government Department of State for Finance and Economic Affairs (DOSFEA), Local Government Area (LGA), parastatals (i.e. government corporations), private employers, households and donors (rest-of-the-world).

b) *Financing agents:* Institutions or entities that channel funds provided by financing sources and use those funds to pay for, or purchase, the activities inside the health accounts boundary (i.e. all activities whose primary purpose is to promote, restore or maintain health). The financing agents in The Gambia include: Department of State for Health and Social Welfare (DoSH), Department of State for Education (DoSE), Department of State for Defence (DoSD), Department of State for Interior (DoSI), DOSFA, LGA, National Aids

Secretariat (NAS), Parastatals, private insurance, households, non-governmental organizations (NGOs), and private firms. The sum of the funds channelled through all the financing agents should be equal to the total amount of money provided by the financing sources.

c) *Providers:* Entities that receive money in exchange for or in anticipation of producing the activities inside the health accounts boundary. Examples of providers in The Gambia include: teaching hospital, general hospitals, private hospitals/clinics, Government Health Centres (Basic Health Services), NGO health centres, pharmacies, opticians, pharmaceutical companies, administration of public health, provision of public health services, other (private insurance), all other providers of health administration, insurance firms, research institutions, education and training institutions, NGO health related activities, and rest of the world. Ideally, the sum of the funds received by all the providers should be equal to the total amount of money provided by the financing agents.

d) *Functions:* Services of curative care, services of rehabilitative care, ancillary services to medical care, medical goods dispensed to out-patients, prevention and public health services, health administration and health insurance, and health related functions. The latter includes: capital formation of health care provider institutions, maintenance service management, education and training of health personnel, research and development in health, traditional medicine development, and provision of overseas treatment.

e) *Resource/input costs:* The factors or inputs used by providers or financing agents to produce the goods and services consumed or the activities conducted in the health system. In The Gambia resource/input cost categories would include: personnel (remuneration, employers contribution employees insurance, other conditions); goods and services (travel and subsistence expenses, drugs and medical supplies, material supplies, transport, utilities, maintenance, property rental and related charges; education and training (research and development, nutritional surveillance, water and sanitation, other services and expenses); subsidies and other current transfers (membership fees and subscription, government organization, individuals and non profit, public and departmental enterprise); and development expenditure (furniture and office equipment; vehicles, operational equipment, machinery).

f) Beneficiaries: The people who receive those health goods and services or benefit from those activities (beneficiaries can be categorized in many different ways, including their age and sex, their socio-economic status, their health status, and their location).

NHA uses many matrix tables for analysis, but due to paucity of data, a decision was made to attempt completing only the following four main matrices: Financing Sources (FS) to Financing Agent (FA): (FS X FA); Financing Agent (FA) to Providers (P): (FA X P); Providers (P) to Inputs (RC): (P X RC); and Financing Agents (FA) to Health Functions (HF): (HF X FA).

The first table cross-tabulates health expenditure by financing source and type of financing agent (FS x FA). This table highlights resource mobilization patterns in the health system. It addresses the question "where does the money come from" by showing the financing sources that contribute to each financing agent. It also shows how prominent a role each source plays in the financing of each financing agent and in the total spending overall.

The second table cross-tabulates health expenditure by the type of financing agent and type of provider (FA x P). This table describes how funds are distributed across different types of providers, e.g., what share of total spending goes to referral and district hospitals relative to hospitals, clinics, health posts, outreach stations.

The third table cross-tabulates health expenditure by provider and type of function (P x F). This table shows how expenditures on different health functions are channelled through the various types of providers. It provides useful perspective on the contribution of different types of providers to the total spending on specific types of services, e.g. public health programmes vis-à-vis secondary and tertiary curative care.

The fourth table cross-tabulates health expenditure by type of financing agent and type of function (FA x F). This table shows who finances what types of services in the health system. It can also highlight the relative emphasis of public and private financing agents with respect to the various public health functions.

2.2. Field Work Methodology

In November 2005, the DOHSW constituted a NHA Technical Working Group (TWG) comprising of the DOHSW, The Gambia Bureau of Statistics

(GBoS), Office of the Directorate of Treasury, Local Consultant, and Head Department of Economist University of The Gambia to undertake a comprehensive NHA study for the years 2002, 2003 and 2004. In addition, the DOHSW constituted a NHA Advisory/Steering Committee to oversee the work of the TWG. The study was coordinated by the Directorate of Planning and Information, with the support of WHO and UNDP FASE Project. The launching of the NHA was done by Permanent Secretary Department of State for Health and Social Welfare.

To facilitate the data collection process a National Health Account sensitization workshop was held in September 2006. Potential NHA stakeholders were invited to a one day workshop where they were introduced to NHA, the usefulness of NHA and its relevance to The Gambia. Another more detailed training workshop was held with the members of NHA TWG. It was in the latter workshop that the generic data collection instruments were adapted for use in Sierra Leone.

The Gambia NHA study relied on secondary and primary data. A wide range of data was collated from various government publications and other sources. For example, to determine household expenditure on health for this exercise, two sources were utilized. In view of the high cost involved in conducting large scale household surveys, it was decided to largely utilize data from the 2003 Integrated Household Survey (IHS) to arrive at estimates of household expenditure on health and also to conduct a small scale household survey in 2006 to address issues of health seeking behaviour which were largely not covered by the IHS.

The IHS from which household health expenditure and utilization rate was obtained, consisted of a sample of 4800 households was drawn across all Local Government Areas LGA) with the probability of selecting a household in an LGA proportional to the size of the LGA, in terms of population. The sampling was done in two levels: enumeration areas (EAs) and households. EAs were stratified by rural-urban areas (12 strata + Banjul and Kanifing).

The Household Health Expenditure and Utilization Survey (HHEUS) conducted in 2006 targeted 1000 households distributed across LGAs. Probability of selecting a household from each of the LGAs was proportional to the population size of the LGA. For the purpose of selecting the sample EA the country was stratified into urban and rural. For the 38 enumeration areas selected for the survey 18 were in urban areas and the remaining 20 in rural areas. As was the case with the IHS the EAs in the 2003 Population and Housing Census were used as the sampling frame. The second stage of the sampling involved the selection of households for the detail interviews. Upon

Table 1. Breakdown of data sources contacted and respondents

	Total number contacted	Number of Responded	Percentage collected
Health Care Providers			
Public	41	41	100
Private/NGO	21	18	86
Sources			
Govt Department	5	5	100
LGAs	8	7	87.5
Donor	17	14	82
NGO	37	20	54
Insurance	4	1	25
Employer/Private firms	73	70	96
Households (2006)	1000	1000	100

the updating of the households in the selected enumeration areas, enumerators selected 25-29 households in each of the selected households. This selection process involved the use of random number table to avoid any bias in the selection.

For the HHEUS data collection 4 teams, each consisting of a supervisor and five enumerators, were constituted. Two officials one from the Central Statistics Department and one from DPI coordinated the data collection. The data collection lasted 20 days. Following the completion of the data collection a coding and editing exercise was undertaken after which using data was entered using the CSPro software. After the entry the data was cleaned of errors and the tables generated.

In addition, to the household survey data, other data was collected from governmental and non-governmental organizations using specially designed NHA survey instruments/questionnaires. The lists of organisations (employers, donors, NGOs, health care providers) were obtained from various registration sources including the Registrar General's Department, The Gambia Chamber of Commerce, NGO Affairs Agency, DoSFA and The Gambia Bureau of Statistics. All identified organisations were included in the survey. A total of 73 private firms, 21 private/NGO health facilities, 37 NGOs, 17 donors and 4 insurance companies were identified for the survey. Table 1 shows the numbers and percentages of different organizations contacted and those that responded. In general the response was high.

After checking for completeness of the questionnaires filled by various organizations, the data were entered, cleaned and preliminary analysis done using Excel software. This data was then entered into dummy matrix tables and analyzed using Excel software. The matrices were built in accordance to the International Classification of NHA (WHO 2003) to facilitate international comparison, but customised to the local situation.

2.3. Limitations of the NHA Study

The study had a number of limitations:

(a) In the 2006 survey household sample size was very small.
(b) Poor response from the Bilateral donors and private health care providers.
(c) Expenditure data from some respondents was not in the NHA questionnaire format.
(d) The IHS questionnaire was not designed to fulfil NHA data needs.
(e) Pledged funding support from other partners was never made available.
(f) NAS could only provide the 2004 data.
(g) Complete expenditure on CISP (Italian Project) was not available.
(h) Expenditure on utility and telecommunication for DOSH were not available.
(i) The health insurance data was available in aggregate form and from only one provider.

3. RESULTS

3.1. Health Financing by Sources

3.1.1. Total Health Expenditure and per Capita Total Health Expenditure

Figure 1 provides total health expenditure (THE) by various sources, including the DOSFEA, LGA, parastatal funds, private employer funds, household funds, and the rest of the world (Donors). THE was Dalasi (GMD) 1,185,223,103 in 2002; GMD 1,395,958,522 in 2003; and GMD 1,682,323,673 in 2004. The Gambia GMD exchange rate against US Dollar

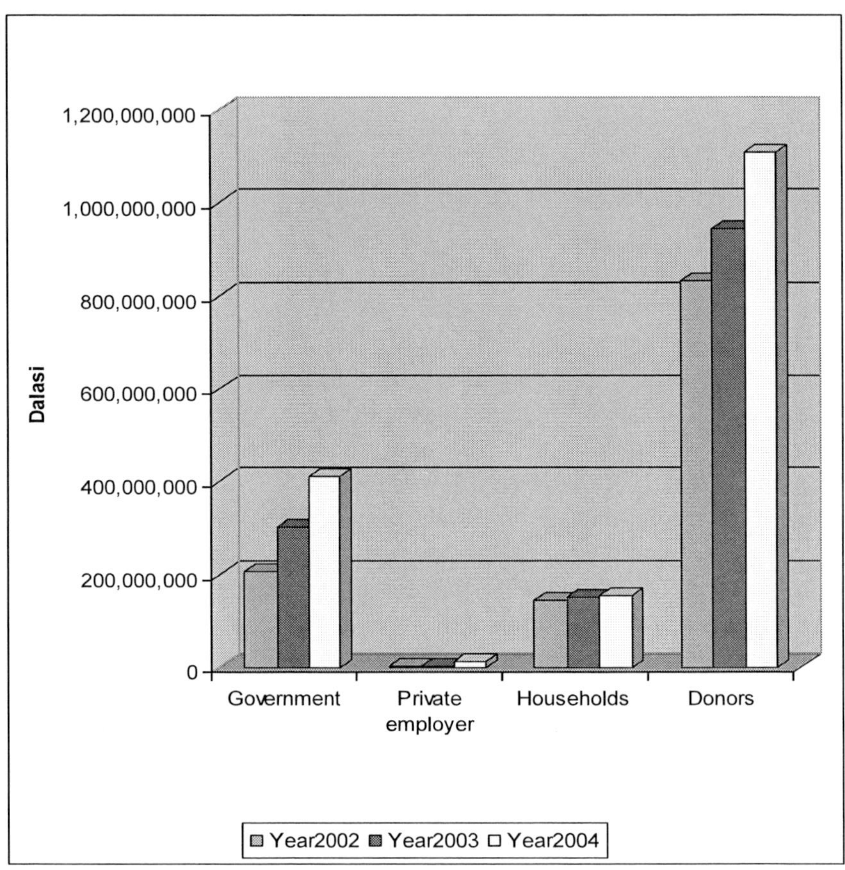

Figure 1. Health expenditure in The Gambia by sources.

was 38.1 in 2002, 32.3 in 2003 and 30.3 in 2004. Total expenditure on health as a percentage of GDP in The Gambia was 16.1% in 2002, 13.9% in 2003 and 14.9% in 2004.

The per capita THE was derived by dividing THE for each year by respective population (1324393 people in year 2002, 1360681 people in year 2003 and 1397964 people in year 2004) estimates from The Gambia Bureau of Statistics (GBS). That yielded a per capita THE of GMD 895 (US$23.5) in 2002, GMD 1026 (US$26.9) in 2003 and GMD 1203 (US$31.6) in 2004. Thus, there was 41.9% nominal growth in the per capita THE between years 2002 and 2004. However, the country had not met the recommendation of the WHO Commission for Macroeconomics and Health (CMH) to spend at least

US$34 per person per year for scaling up a set of essential health interventions (WHO 2001). During the years under consideration, it was only Cape Verde that met the CMH recommendation.

Figure 2 shows the per capita THE for the 15 ECOWAS countries (WHO 2006). During the three years, per capita THE for The Gambia was higher than that of Guinea-Bissau, Liberia, Niger, Sierra Leone and Togo, but lower than that of the remaining ECOWAS countries.

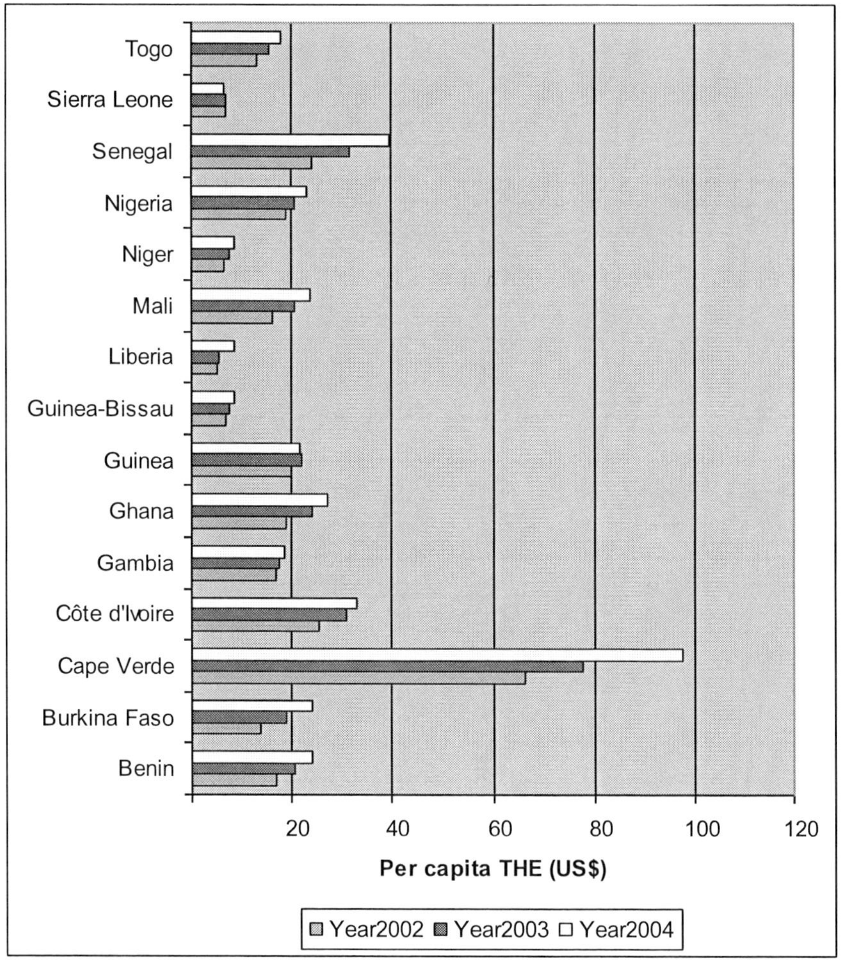

Figure 2. Per capita total health expenditure (THE) for ECOWAS.

3.1.2. Total Health Expenditure by Source

There are broadly four sources of health financing in the Gambia, namely: public/government, household out-of-pocket payments (OOPs), private employers and donors (rest of the world). This subsection provides a distribution THE by each of those sources. *Figure 3* shows a breakdown of heath financing by source in The Gambia for year 2002. Out of the THE of GMD 1185223103 in 2002, 70.2% came from donors, 17.5% from government/public, 12.2% from household OOPs, and 0.1% from private employers

Figure 4 presents an analysis of heath financing by source in The Gambia for year 2003. During that year THE was GMD 1395958522, of which 67.6% were from donors, 21.6% from government/public, 10.7% from household OOPs and 0.1% from private employers.

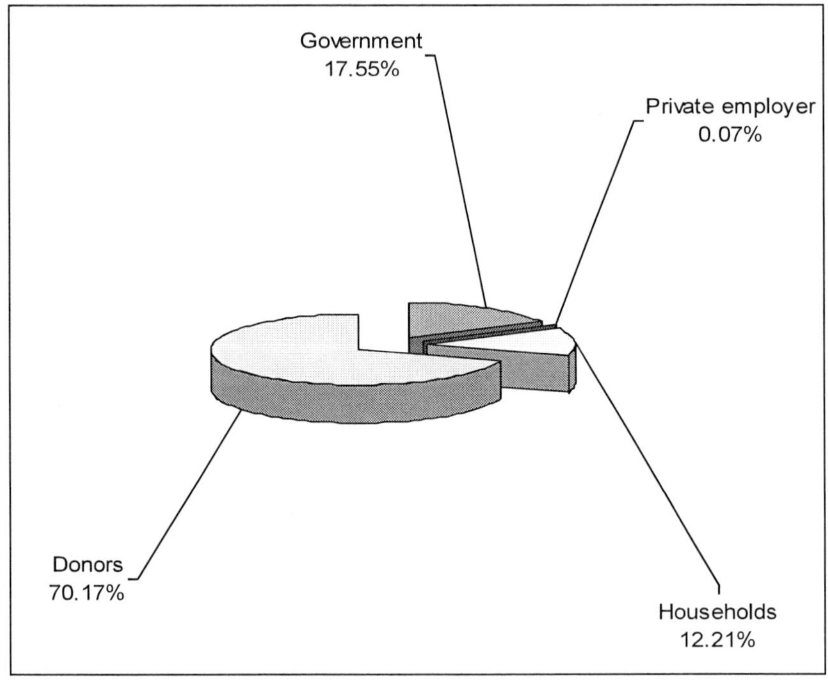

Figure 3. Health financing by source in The Gambia, 2002.

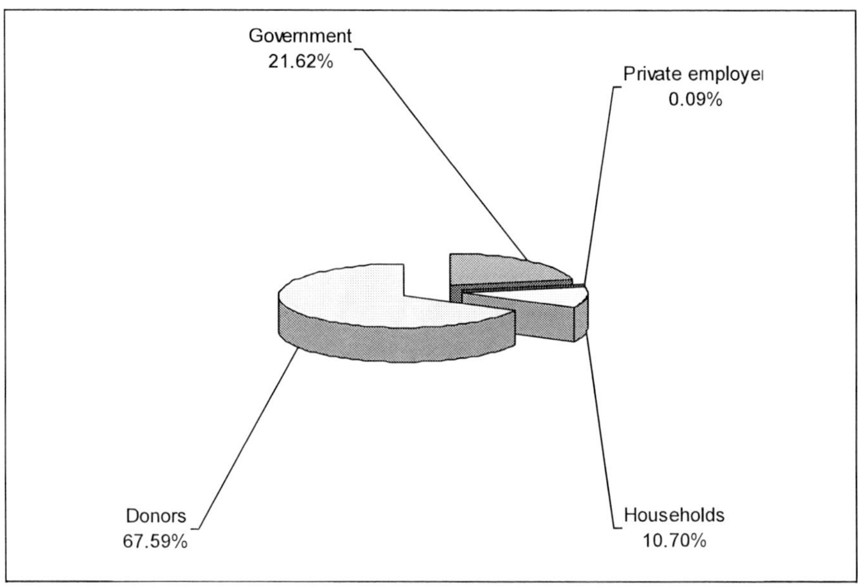

Figure 4. Health financing by source in The Gambia, 2003.

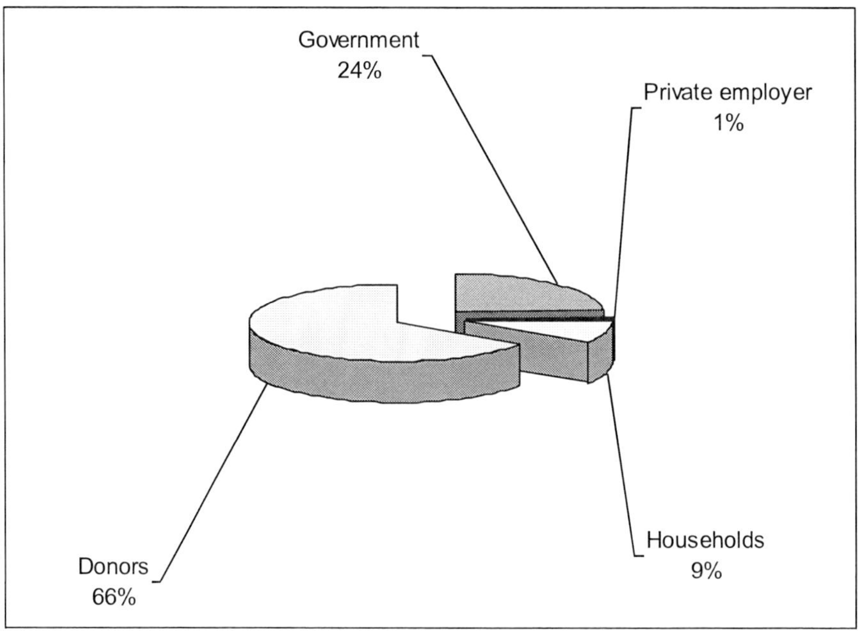

Figure 5. Health financing by source in The Gambia, 2004.

Figure 5 shows an itemization of heath financing by source in The Gambia for year 2004. In 2004 THE was GMD 1682323673, of which 65.9% originated from donors, 24.6% from government/public, 9.2% from household OOPs, and 0.7% from private employer funds.

It is clear that majority of health funds came from the rest of the world (donors). However, there is evidence that the donor and household funding as a percentage of THE decreased slightly between years 2002 and 2004. The funding from private employers remained fairly constant.

Government Health Expenditure on Health: General government expenditure on health (GGHE) includes health expenditure at all levels (and ministries) of government, including the expenditure of public corporations. In the GGHE consists of funding from DoSFEA, LGA and parastatals. The total GGHE was GMD 207,995,042.6 (18% of THE) in year 2002; GMD 301,763,059 (22% of THE) in 2003; and GMD 409,165,197.14 (24% of THE) in 2004. During the three years majority of GGHE came from DoSFEA (93%), parastatals (6%), and LGA (1%). Approximately 34.2%, 24.1% and 40.4% of the GGHE was from external loans in years 2002, 2003 and 2004 respectively.

The per capita GGHE for The Gambia was GMD 691 in 2002, GMD 812 in 2003 and GMD 975 in 2004. *Figure 6* portrays the per capita government health expenditure on health in the ECOWAS. The per capita GGHE was less than US$10 in Cote D'Ivoire, The Gambia, Guinea, Guinea-Bissau, Liberia, Niger, Nigeria, Sierra Leone and Togo.

The Gambian government expenditure on health as a percentage of total government expenditure was 11.47% in year 2002, 13.03% in 2003 and 10.86% in 2004. *Figure 7* shows the GGHE as a percentage of total government expenditure.

In the Abuja Declaration, Heads of States and Governments of the African Union set a target of allocating at least 15% of their annual national budget to the improvement of the health sector (OAU 2001). In 2004 Cote D'Ivoire, Guinea, Guinea-Bissau, and Nigeria spent less than 5% of their total government expenditure on health. According to the World Health Report (WHO 2006), it was only Burkina Faso and Liberia that had met the Heads of State target as at the end of year 2004. This means the 13 ECOWAS countries that spent less than 15% of their national budgets on health will need to take appropriate steps to honour the commitment made by their respective Heads of State.

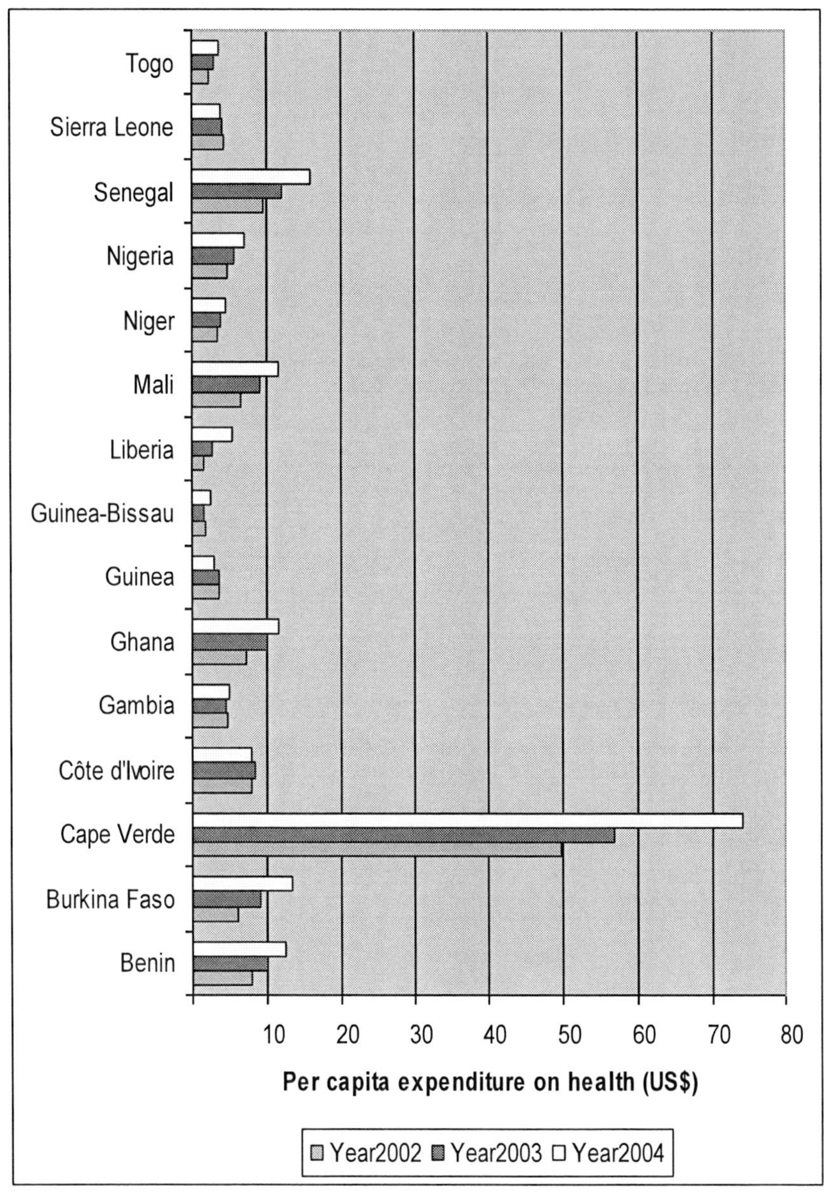

Figure 6. Per capita government expenditure on health in ECOWAS.

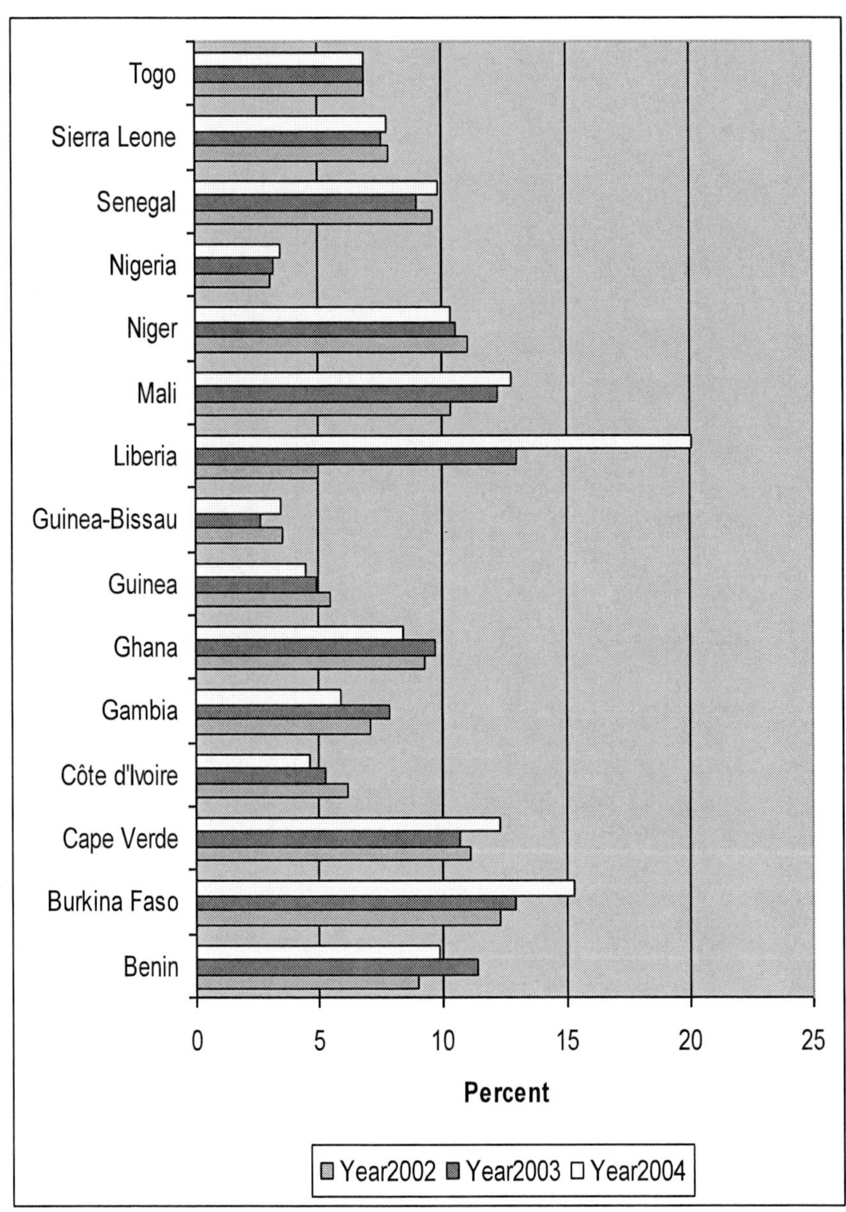

Figure 7. Government expenditure on health as a percentage of total government expenditure.

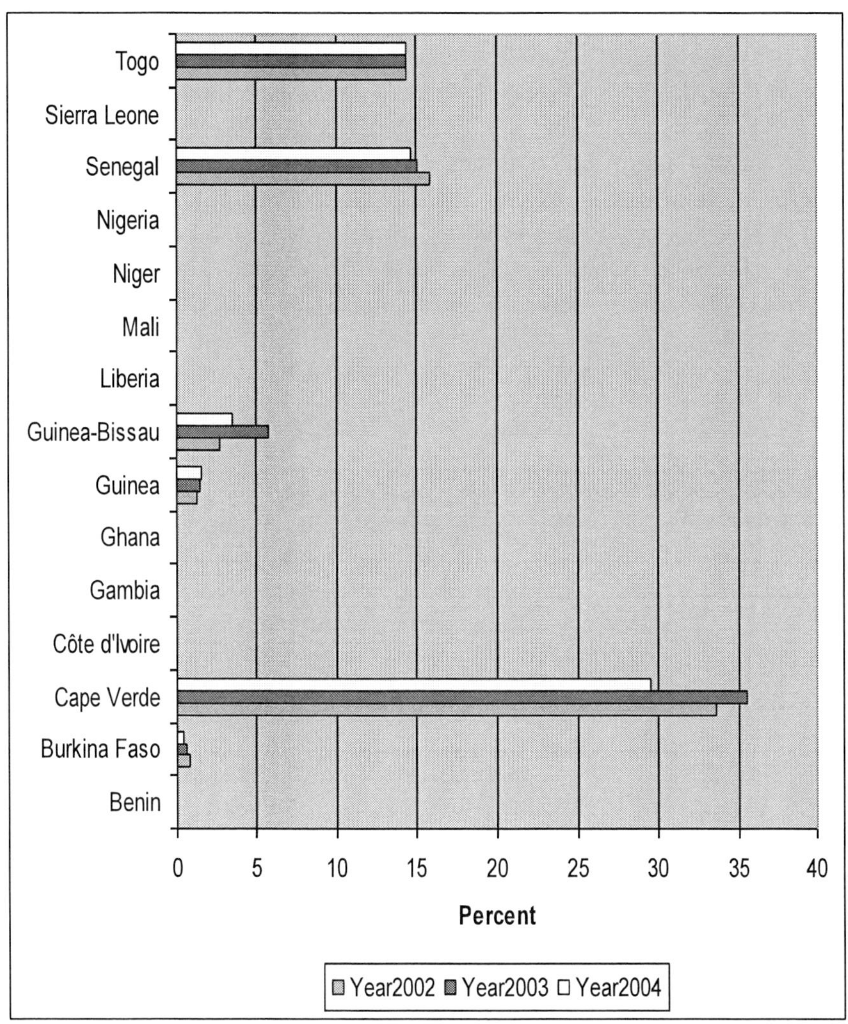

Figure 8. Social security expenditure on health as a percentage of general government expenditure on health in ECOWAS.

Social security spending on health: NHA guidelines define social security schemes as "social insurance schemes covering the community as a whole or large sections of the community that are imposed and controlled by government units. They generally involve compulsory contributions by employees or employers or both, and the terms on which benefits are paid to recipients are determined by government units. The schemes cover a wide variety of programmes, providing benefits in cash or in kind for old age, invalidity or death, survivors, sickness and maternity, work injury, unemployment, family allowance, health care, etc. There is usually no link between the amount of the contribution paid by an individual and the risk to which that individual is exposed [p.302]" (WHO 2003).

In The Gambia, Benin, Cote D'Ivoire, Ghana, Liberia, Mali, Niger, Nigeria, and Sierra Leone social security did not contribute to the general government expenditure on health. In the remaining six ECOWAS countries social security contributed to health spending. Social security spending on health constituted over 14% of GGEH in Cape Verde, Senegal and Togo (see *Figure 8*).

3.1.3. Private Expenditure on Health

Private health financing includes spending by private insurance, private households' out-of-pocket payment (OOPs), non-profit institutions (other than social insurance), and private firms and employers (WHO 2003). Private financing for health comes from personal out-of-pocket payments made directly to various providers (e.g. public health facilities, private practitioners, private pharmacists, and traditional healers), prepayments to private insurance and indirect payments for health services by employers (firms) and local charitable groups.

The total private health expenditure on health in The Gambia was GMD 145,545,671 in year 2002; GMD 150,610,801; and GMD 165,222,560. Private spending constituted 12.3% of the THE in 2002, 10.8% in 2003 and 9.8% in The Gambia in 2004. Private expenditure on health as a percentage of THE has not changed much over the three years. This source consists of primarily OOPs and private health insurance (prepaid plans). The per capita private health expenditure was GMD 128.4 in year 2002, GMD 145.5 in 2003 and GMD 156.7 in 2004.

Figure 9 shows private spending on health as a percentage of the total expenditure on health for ECOWAS countries. This figure was generated from the NHA estimated contained in the World Heath Report 2006 (WHO 2006). In that report the private health spending for The Gambia appears to have been over estimated.

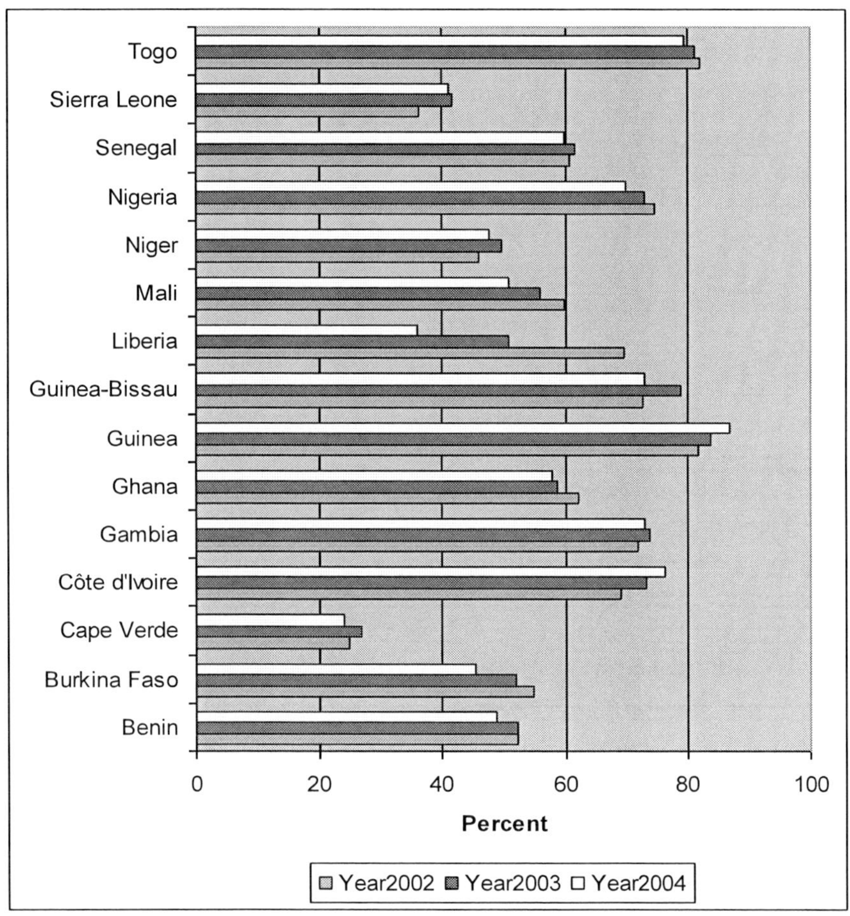

Figure 9. Private expenditure on health as a percentage of total expenditure on health in ECOWAS.

In 2002, out of a total private health expenditure in The Gambia of GMD 145545671, 99.46% came from household funds and 0.54% from private employers. In 2003 the private health expenditure on health was GMD 150,610,801 – 99.18% from household funds and 0.82% from private employers. In 2004 the private health expenditure on health was GMD 165,222,560 – 93.32% from household funds and 6.68% from private employers.

Out-of-pocket payments (OOPs): In 2002 household OOPs constituted 99.46% of the private health expenditure; 99.18% in 2003; and 93.32% in 2004. It is evident that the households, through direct out-of-pocket

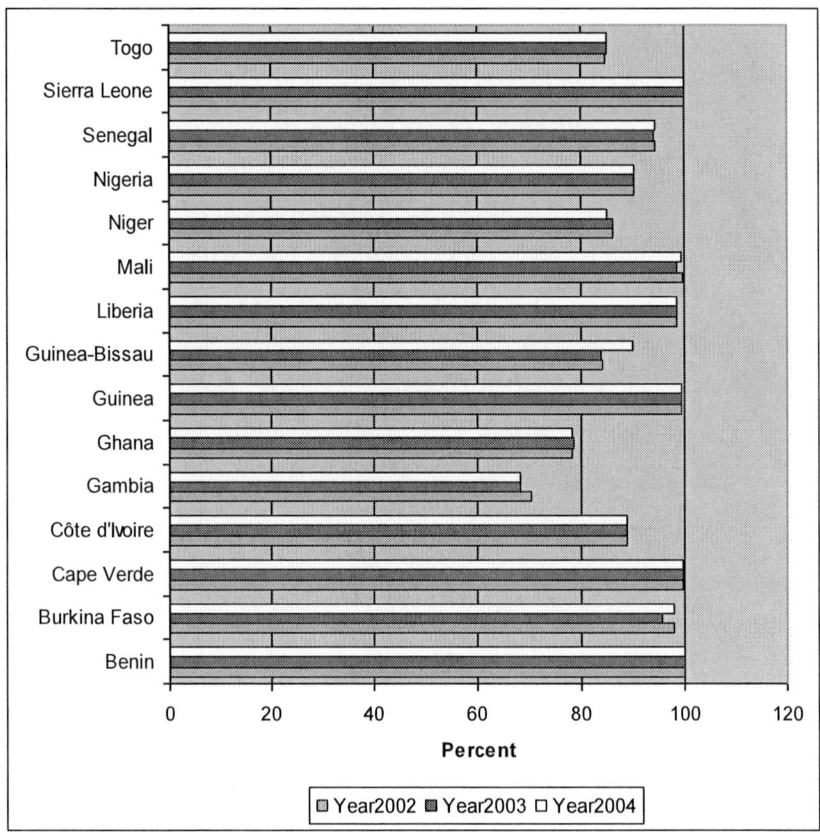

Figure 10. Out-of-pocket expenditure as a percentage of private health expenditure on health.

expenditures at the point of service consumption, make a significant contribution to the private health expenditure in The Gambia. *Figure 10* shows OOPs on health as a percentage of private expenditure on health for ECOWAS countries. Except for Ghana, household OOPs accounted for over 80% of private health expenditure on health.

Private prepaid plans: Figure 11 presents private prepaid plans (which are voluntary in nature) as a percentage of private expenditure on health. Apparently, The Gambia, Guinea, Guinea-Bissau, Liberia and Sierra Leone health systems did not receive any funding from prepaid plans. Contrastingly, the private prepaid plans accounted for more than 10% of private expenditure on health in Cote D'Ivoire and Niger.

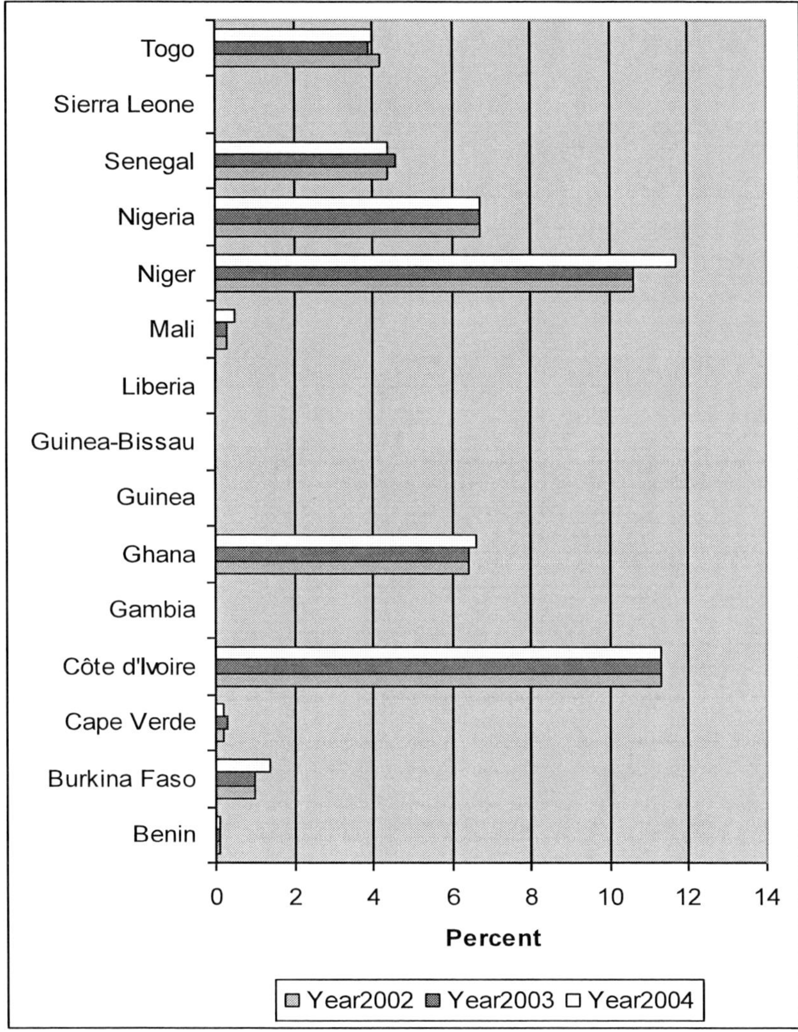

Figure 11. Private prepaid plans as a percentage of private expenditure on health in ECOWAS.

External financing: External resources for health consist of mainly of grants from multilateral and bilateral aid donors and international nongovernmental organisations (e.g. Global Fund for AIDS, Tuberculosis and Malaria). Donors made a contribution of GMD 831,682,389 to health in 2002

(70.2%); GMD 943,584,662 (67.6%) in 2003; and GMD 1,107,935,916 (65.9%) in 2004. Thus, donors are a majority contributor to THE in The Gambia.

Figure 12 shows external resources for health as a percentage of total expenditure on health. The figure has been generated from the World Health Report 2006. Once again it is clear that donor contribution to THE in The Gambia was significantly higher than reported in the World Health Report. Donors contribute more than 20% of THE in 8 (53%) ECOWAS countries.

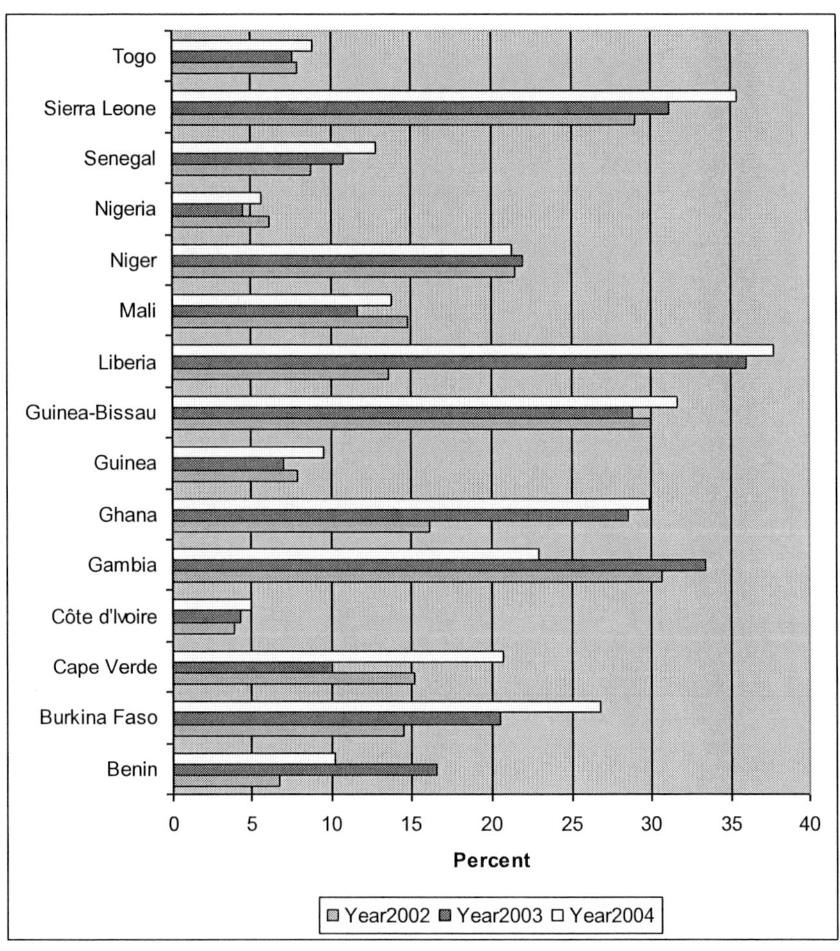

Figure 12. External resources for health as a percentage of total expenditure on health in ECOWAS.

3.2. Health Financing by Financing Agents

There were four categories of financing agents, namely: government (public), private, and external. *Figure 13* depicts the distribution of funds between public, private and external financing agents. Clearly the public financing agents absorbed the majority of health financing over the three year period. It is also vivid that the funds going into the public health financing agents grew consistently over the period under consideration. The funding to the private financing agents grew by a small margin.

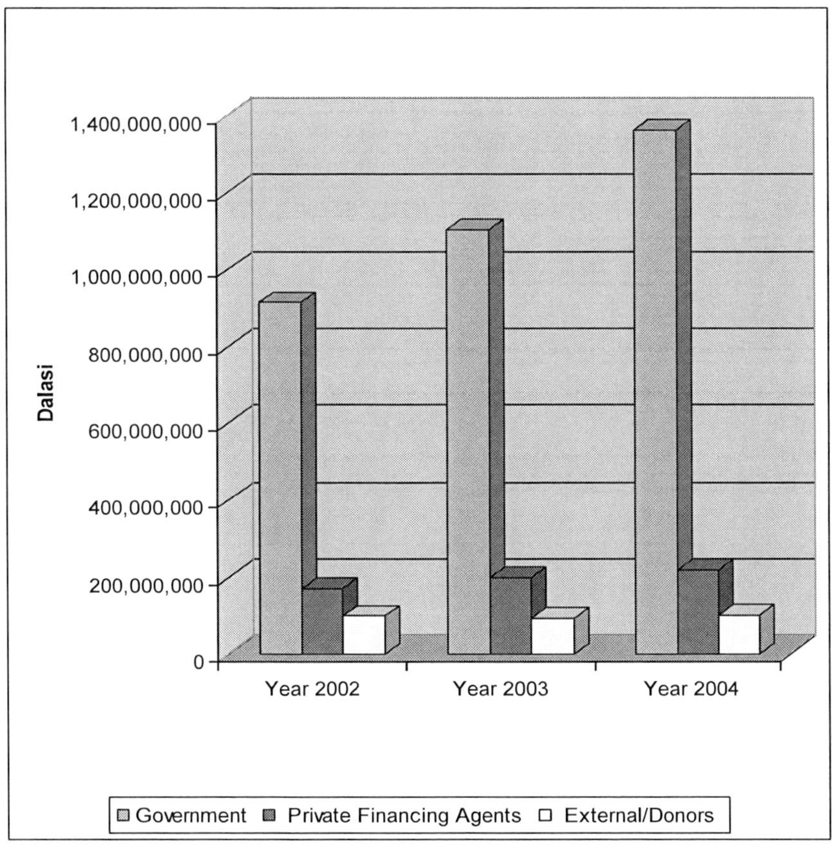

Figure 13. Funds received by public, private and external financing agents in The Gambia.

3.2.1. Public Health Financing Agents

The public financing agents consisted of DoSH, DoSE, DoSD, DoSI, DoSFA, LGA, National AIDS Secretariat, NaNA and parastatals. In 2002 the public financing agents received GMD 915,547,949.8; of which 96.03% went to DOSH, 0.13% to DOSE, 0.00% to DoSD, 0.05% to DoSI, 3.39% to DoSFA, 0.36% to LGA and 0.04% to NaNA (See *Figure 14*).

In 2003 the public financing agents received GMD 1,104,213,908.12; of which 96.70% to DoSH, 0.12% to DoSE, 0.00% to DoSD, 0.04% to DoSI, 2.81% to DoSFA, 0.30% to LGA and 0.03% to NaNA (See *Figure 15*).

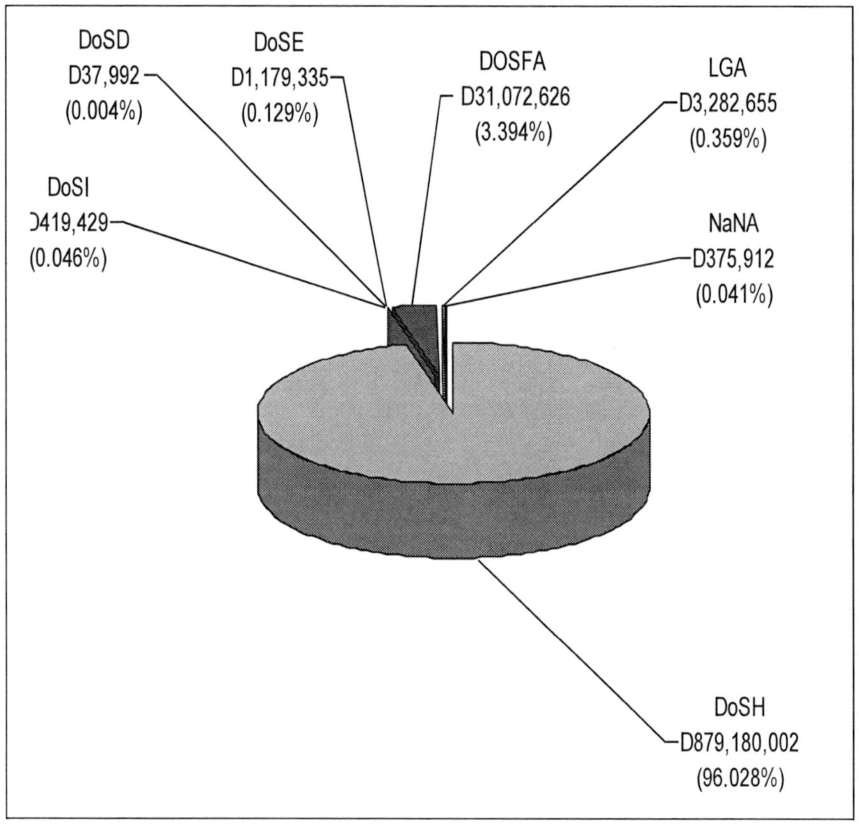

Figure 14. Gambia funding to public health financing agents, 2002.

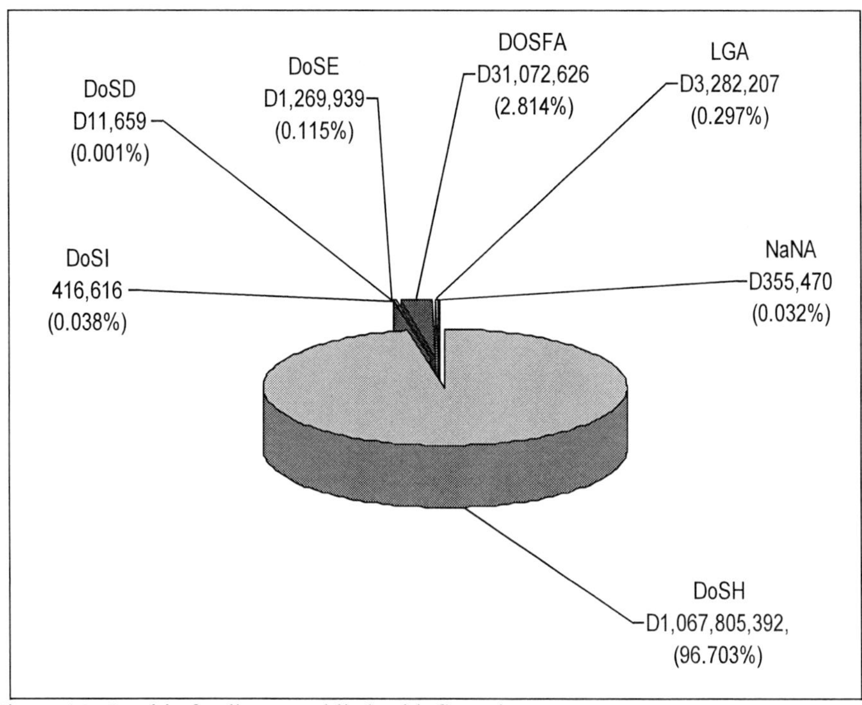

Figure 15. Gambia funding to public health financing agents, 2003.

In 2004 the public financing agents received GMD 1,362,716,725.87; of which 88.59% to DoSH, 0.16% to DoSE, 0.04% to DoSI, 2.81% to DoSFA, 0.32% to LGA, 8.55% to NAS, and 0.06% to NaNA (See *Figure 16*). It is evident in Figures 14 to 16 that majority of health financing that went to the public health sector were spent by health service providers within the aegis of the Department of State for Health.

3.2.2. Private Health Financing Agents
The private financing agents included private insurance, household out-of-pocket payments, non-governmental organizations, and private firms. *Figure 17* portrays The Gambia's funding to the private health financing agents in year 2002. Eighty-five percent of funds received by private health financing agents were administered by households; 7% by NGOs; 4% by private firms; and 4% by private insurance.

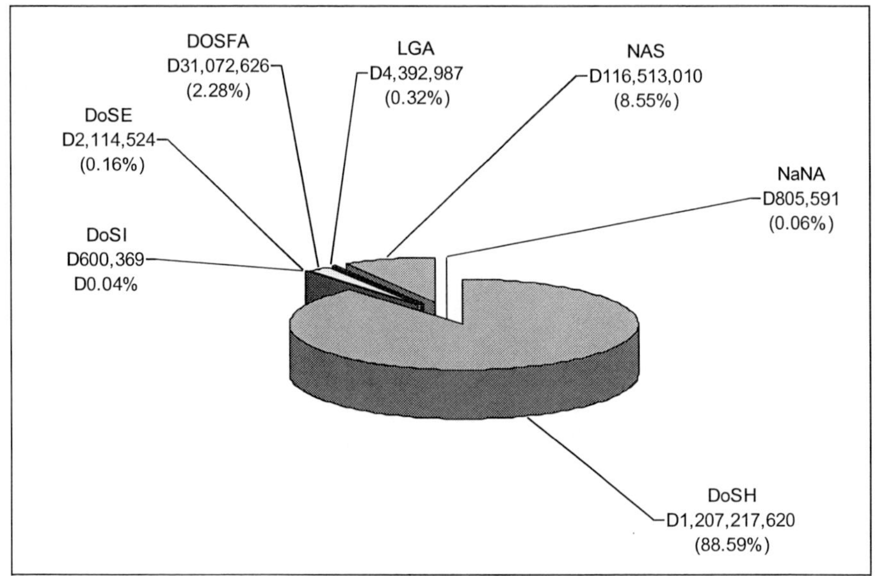

Figure 16. Gambia funding to public health financing agents, 2004.

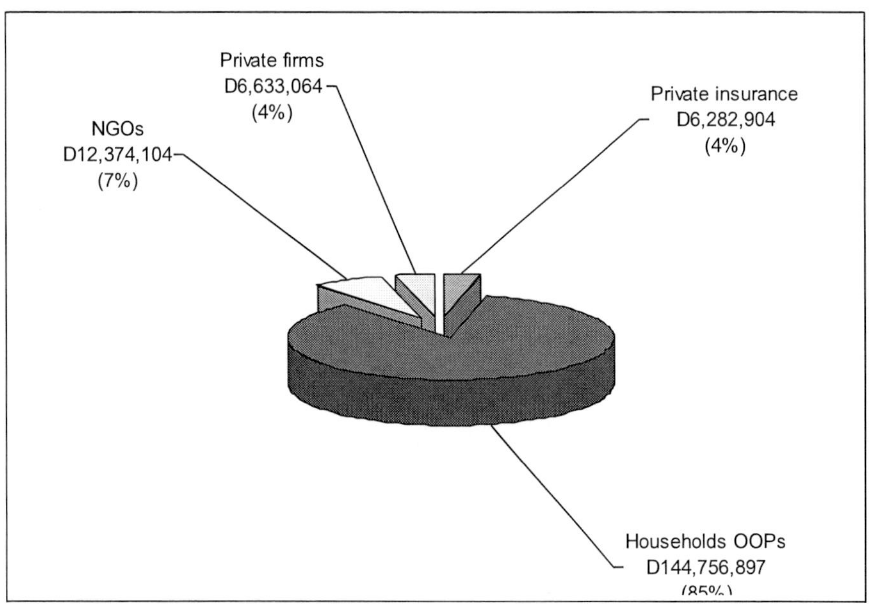

Figure 17. Gambia funding to private health agents, 2002.

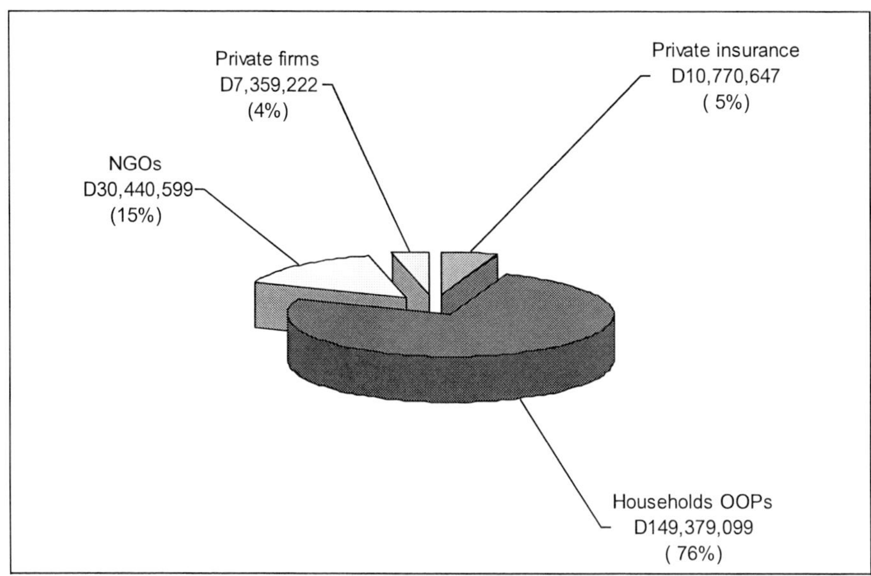

Figure 18. Gambia funding to private health financing agents, 2003.

Figure 18 presents The Gambia's funding to the private health financing agents in year 2003. Seventy-six percent of funds received by private health financing agents were administered by households; 15% by NGOs; 4% by private firms; and 5% by private insurance.

Figure 19 presents The Gambia's funding to the private health financing agents in year 2004. Seventy percent of funds received by private health financing agents were administered by households; 18% by NGOs; 7% by private firms; and 5% by private insurance.

Evidence contained in Figures 17 to 19 vividly shows that majority of the health funds received by private financing agents were used by households to purchase health services from various service providers in The Gambia.

3.2.3. External Financing Agent

The external financing agent consisted of rest of the world (donors). *Figure 20* presents the total funds received by the rest of the world entities operating within The Gambia. The trend has not been consistent across the three year period.

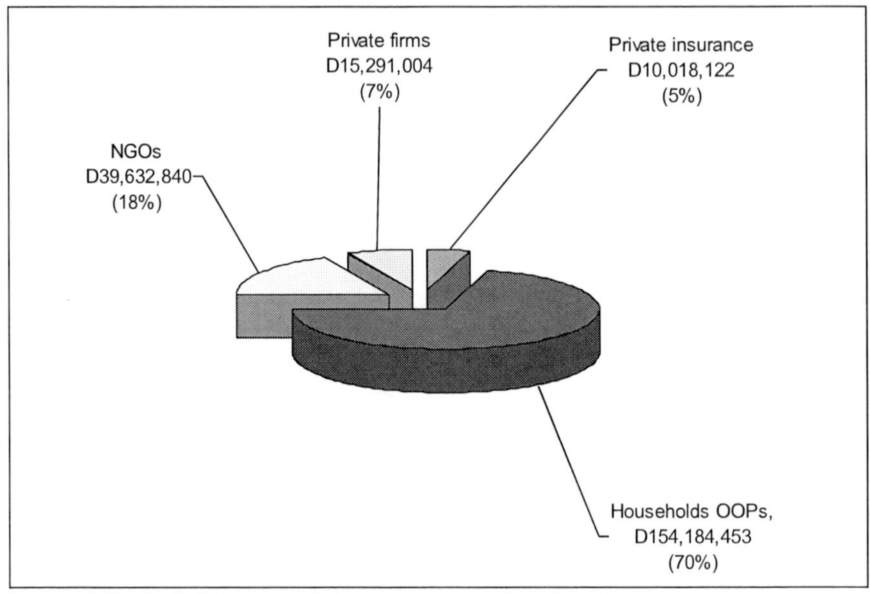

Figure 19. Gambia funding to private health insurance agents, 2004.

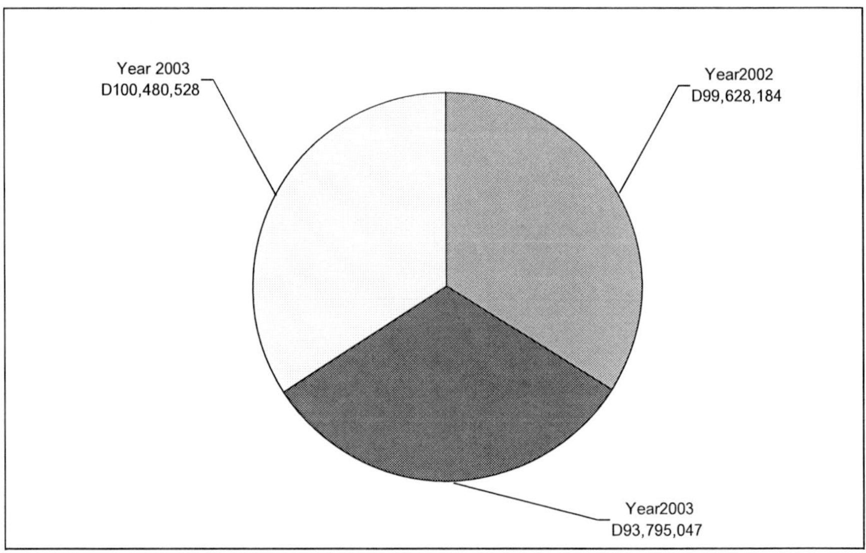

Figure 20. Funds received by the rest of the world in Gambia.

3.3. Distribution of Health Funds from Financing Agents to Providers

Figure 21 presents the distribution of health funds from financing agents to health service providers in 2002. Out of the total health expenditure of GMD 1185223103, approximately 53% was spent on provision and administration of public health programmes, 18% on hospitals, 18% on institutions providing health related services, 10% on health centres, and 1% on rest of the world.

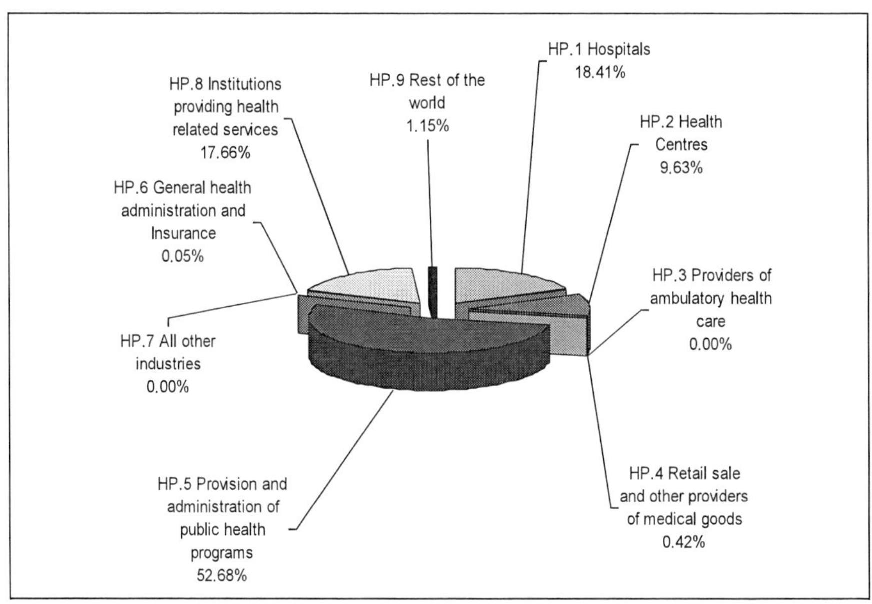

Figure 21. Distribution of funds from financing agents to providers, 2002.

Figure 22 portrays the distribution of health funds from financing agents to health service providers in 2003. Out of the total health expenditure of GMD 1395963523, approximately 48% was spent on provision and administration of public health programmes, 24% on hospitals, 16% on institutions providing health related services, 11% on health centres, and 1% on rest of the world.

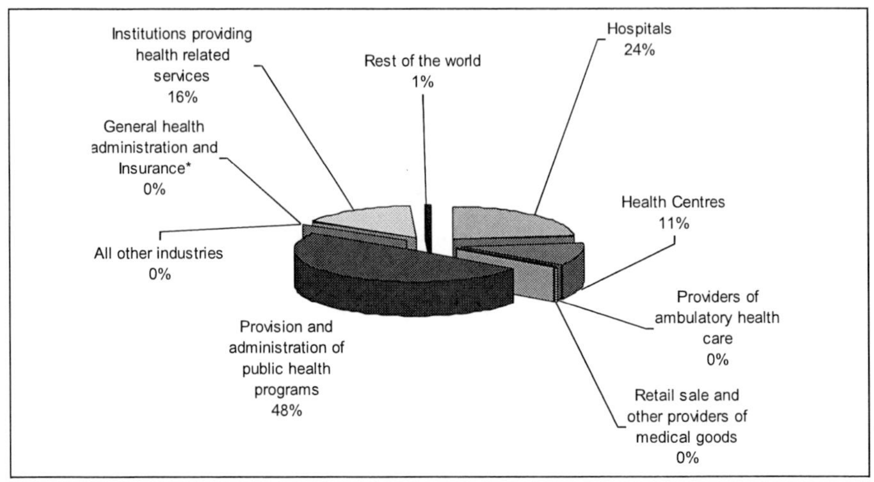

Figure 22. Distribution of funds from financing agents to providers, 2003.

Figure 23 depicts the distribution of health funds from financing agents to health service providers in 2004. Out of the total health expenditure of GMD 1682323673, approximately 57% was spent on provision and administration of public health programmes, 21% on hospitals, 11% on institutions providing health related services, 10% on health centres, and 1% on rest of the world.

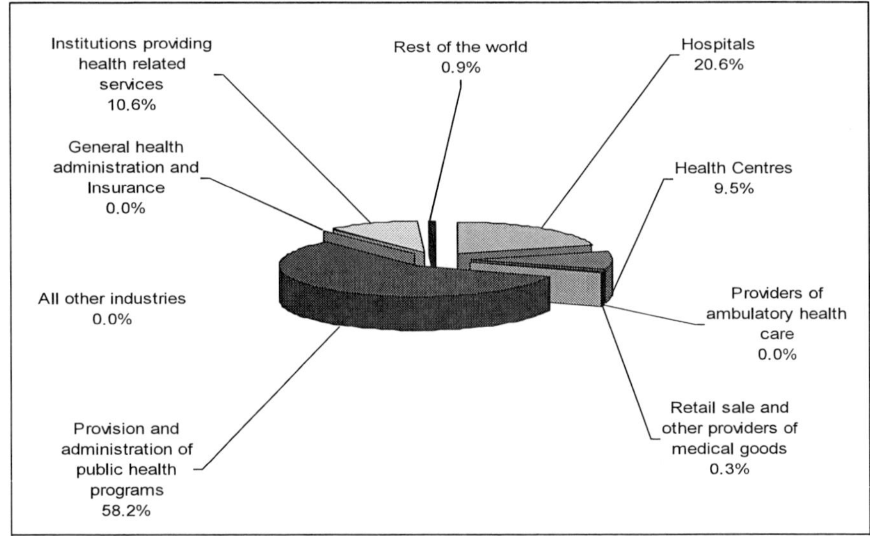

Figure 23. Distribution of funds from financing agents to providers, 2004.

The above distribution of health funds to providers is quite encouraging. In most of the other African countries a critical mass of the THE goes to teaching and general hospitals. Whereas the preferred scenario is where most of the resources are invested in the public health programmes aimed at protecting majority of the population from the risk of illness. In The Gambian case, majority of the total health expenditure rationally goes to the administration and provision of public health services.

3.4. Distribution of Funds from Health Service Providers to Health Functions

Figure 24 shows the flow of health funds from service providers to health functions in 2002. Out of the total health expenditure of GMD 1185223103, approximately 38% was spent on prevention and public health services, 19% on health administration and health insurance, 18% on services of curative care, 18% on health related functions and 7% on medical goods dispensed to outpatients.

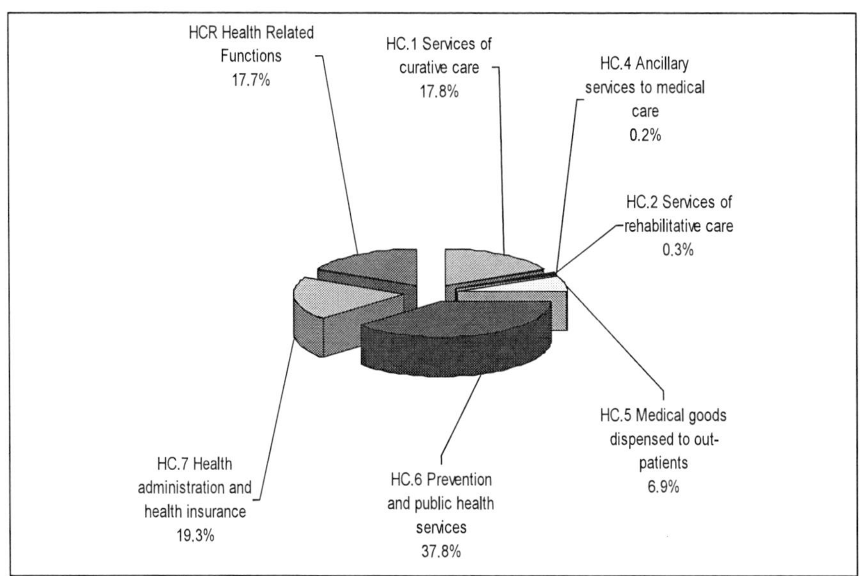

Figure 24. Flow of health care funds from providers to functions, 2002.

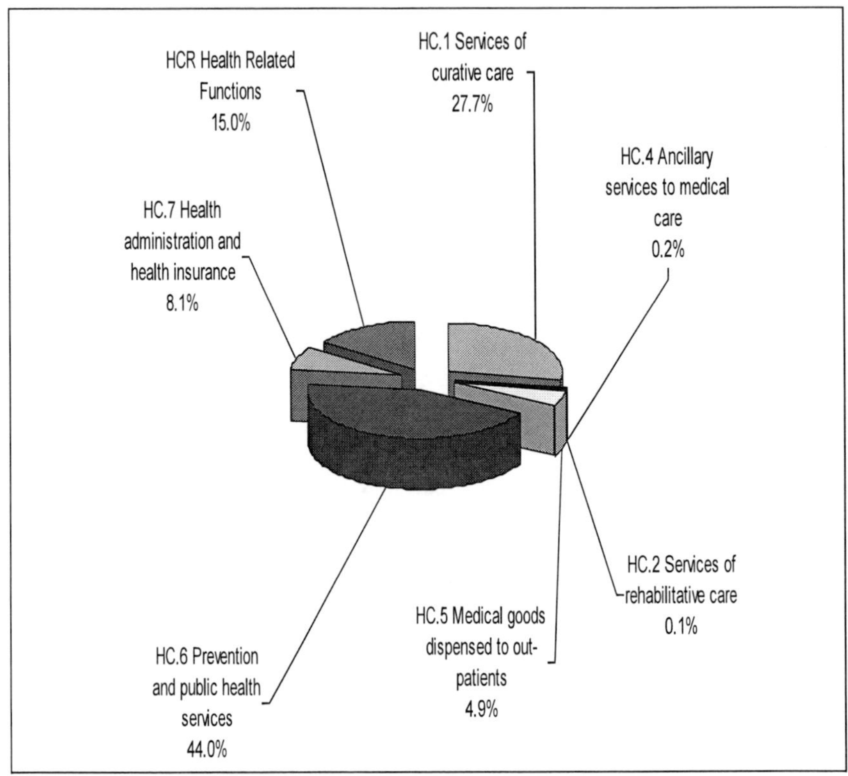

Figure 25. Flow of health care funds from providers to functions, 2003.

Figure 25 displays the flow of health funds from service providers to health functions in 2003. Out of the total health expenditure of GMD 1395963523, approximately 44% was spent on prevention and public health services, 28% on services of curative care, 8% on health administration and health insurance, 15% on health related functions and 5% on medical goods dispensed to outpatients.

Figure 26 demonstrates the flow of health funds from service providers to health functions in 2004. Out of the total health expenditure of GMD 1682323673, approximately 33% on health administration and health insurance, 29% was spent on prevention and public health services, 21% on services of curative care, 13% on health related functions, 3% on medical goods dispensed to outpatients, and 1% on ancillary services to medical care.

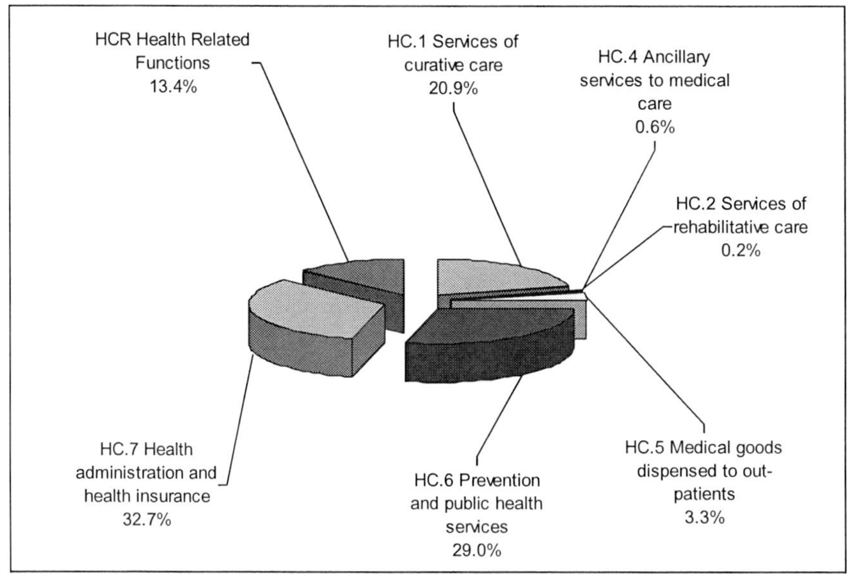

Figure 26. Flow of health care funds from providers to functions, 2004.

4. DISCUSSION

4.1. Key Findings

The total health expenditure (THE) was approximately GMD 1185223103 in 2002; GMD 1395958522 in 2003; and GMD 1682323673 in 2004. THE as a percentage of GDP in The Gambia was 16.1% in 2002, 13.9% in 2003 and 14.9% in 2004. The per capita total health expenditure was GMD 895 in 2002, GMD 1026 in 2003 and GMD 1203 in 2004. During the three years over 66% of the total health funding came from donors (international health development partners). The Government of The Gambia contribution grew from 18% in 2002 to 24% of the total health expenditure in 2004. The households, through direct out-of-pocket payments to health care providers, contributed 12% in 2002, 11% in 2003 and 9% in 2004 to the total health expenditure.

The DoSH should consider developing a comprehensive health financing policy and health financing strategic plan with a roadmap of how the Government plans to realize the vision of universal coverage of health services and universal population protection from potentially catastrophic and impoverishing health care expenditures in the long-term (Kirigia and Diarra-Nama 2008). In the process of developing the national financing policy, it may be informative to refer to both the WHO World Health Report 2010 (WHO 2010) and the WHO regional strategy for health financing (WHO/AFRO 2006) for inspiration. The following important findings should support the development of the health financing policy:

(a) The Gambia per capita total health expenditure is below the average US$34 minimum expenditure for scaling up a set of essential interventions recommended by the WHO Commission for Macroeconomics and Health (WHO 2001). Therefore, the financing policy should advocate for increased government expenditure on health.

(b) Currently Social Security contribution to health is insignificant. The policy should therefore advocate for increase Social security contribution to health expenditure.

(c) The out-of-pocket expenditure as a proportion of total private health expenditure is over 95%. The health financing policy should advocate for the development of a prepaid health financing mechanism (e.g. national social insurance) with inbuilt safety nets for the poor.

(d) Donor contribution to the total health expenditure is over 65%. For effective coordination of this input the health financing policy should advocate for basket funding system. Alternatively, the policy can advocate for general budget support, such that all funds received are channelled through the government treasury for rational allocation to implement the national health policy. The latter may increase the aid effectiveness.

CONCLUSION

The inaugural NHA study reported in this paper was the first step towards The Gambia's aspiration of institutionalizing NHA to facilitate DOSH stewardship of the national health system. The study succeeded in addressing three of its four objectives: (i) to estimate the total health expenditure from public, private and donor sources; (ii) to determine the total health expenditure by financing agents; and (iii) to approximate the distribution of funds by

various public health functions. Due to dearth of disaggregated information, it was not possible to estimate the amounts of funds spent on various health system inputs.

The NHA evidence contained in this document constitutes a good basis for developing a comprehensive health financing policy and a health financing strategic plan mapping out how the Government plans to realize the vision of universal coverage of health services and universal protection from potentially catastrophic and impoverishing health care expenditures in the long-term (WHO 2010). In order to facilitate the monitoring and evaluation of such policy documents once developed, it is important to institutionalize national health accounts. The latter will require boosting of the capacities in the DOSH Directorate of Planning and Information.

ACKNOWLEDGMENTS

We are immensely grateful to The Gambia Department of State for Health and Social Welfare for having authorized and supported the conduct of inaugural National Health Accounts study reported in this article. The support of WHO and UNDP FASE Project towards the NHA study is greatly appreciated. *Lamin Jallow*, before his untimely death in 2009, made an invaluable contribution to the entire NHA study. We owe profound gratitude to the Almighty God for meeting all our needs during the entire process of conducting and writing the study. This article contains the views of the authors only and does not represent the decisions or the stated policies of the institutions they work for.

REFERENCES

Government of the Gambia (1980). *The Gambia primary health care programme.* Banjul: Department of State for Health and Social Welfare.

Government of the Gambia (1988). *Drug revolving fund procedures manual.* Banjul: Department of State for Health and Social Welfare.

Government of the Gambia (2000). *Bamako Initiative procedures manual.* Banjul: Department of State for Health and Social Welfare.

Government of the Gambia (2002). *Health services user fees revised list.* Banjul: Department of State for Health and Social Welfare.

Government of the Gambia (2006). *Health management information systems report.* Banjul: Department of State for Health and Social Welfare.

Kirigia, J.M. & Diarra-Nama. A.J. (2008). *Can countries of the WHO African Region wean themselves off the donor funding for health?* Bulletin of the World Health Organization, 86(11): 889-892.

Organization of African Unity (2001). *Abuja declaration on HIV/AIDS, tuberculosis and other related infectious diseases.* OAU/SPS/Abuja/3. Addis Ababa: OAU.

World Health Organization (2001). *Investing in Health: Report of the WHO Commission for Macroeconomics and Health.* Geneva: WHO.

World Health Organization (2003). *Guide to producing national health accounts: with special applications for low-income and middle-income countries.* Geneva: WHO.

World Health Organization (2006). *The World Health Report 2006: working together for health.* Geneva: WHO.

World Health Organization (2010). *The world health report - Health systems financing: the path to universal coverage.* Geneva: WHO.

In: Health Insurance
Editors: E. Abrahamsen et al.

ISBN: 978-1-62081-050-7
© 2012 Nova Science Publishers, Inc.

Chapter 2

CHANGES IN INSURANCE STATUS OF A COHORT PUBLIC MENTAL HEALTH CLIENTS IN UTRECHT AFTER THE INTRODUCTION OF A NEW HEALTH INSURANCE SYSTEM: THE IMPACT OF INTENSIFIED CASE MANAGEMENT

R. B. J. Smit, A. P. L. van Bergen
and E. J. C. van Ameijden
Municipal Health Service Utrecht, Utrecht, The Netherlands

ABSTRACT

The Netherlands has a long tradition of health insurance based on the combination of both social and private insurance systems respectively. On January 1 2006 a new Health Insurance Act (Zorgverzekeringswet) (HIA), came into force. Under this Act all residents of the Netherlands are legally obliged to take out a basic health insurance which covers standard medical expenses such as General Practitioner, hospitals costs or pharmaceutical costs. As in many countries, vulnerable groups such as the homeless and those addicted to drugs and alcohol, are often uninsured for the cost of medical care. With the advent of the new HIA, it was anticipated that higher premium contributions, own risk levels and administrative procedures would lead to an increase in the number of people without adequate health insurance. A lack of health insurance has serious consequences, not only for the individuals concerned, but also for the accessibility, utilisation and quality of healthcare.

In the city of Utrecht, several provisions have been put in place to improve the level of insurance of vulnerable groups and those affected by the Health Insurance Act and to maintain their insurance. In order to evaluate these provisions, the health insurance status of a group of 3,168 Public Mental Health care (PMHc) clients in the city of Utrecht was followed from July 2004 to January 2008, both retrospectively and prospectively. The percentage of uninsured PMHc clients showed a decrease from 27.4% in July 2004 to 12.4% in January 2008. The decrease was most noticeable in the group of addicted persons. However, the decline stagnated in the course of 2008. It was recommended to intensify case management in order to further decrease the proportion of uninsured in this client group. Of the original 2004 cohort, 245 persons had died, 33 had left the country and 178 were not found in any health insurance register. For the remaining cohort members a trend analysis was made. In January 2011 12.0% of the cohort members were uninsured, with higher percentages among persons younger than 40 (15.3%) and non-Dutch clients (13.9%) and a lower percentage among clients with a personal case manager (13.5%). Since case management seems to reduce the proportion of uninsured subjects the recommendation is to continue to focus on and intensify case management across all vulnerable groups.

Keywords: Health Insurance Act, uninsured, socially vulnerable persons, addicts, Public Mental Healthcare, homeless persons.

INTRODUCTION

In the Netherlands some form of health insurance has been in place since the beginning of the 20th century. However, it was only in 1941 that a public health insurance scheme was introduced under the Sickness Fund Decree. A tripartite system was imposed: a compulsory social health insurance scheme for wage earners and their dependents, voluntary social health insurance for self-employed people and a private health insurance. Eligibility for cover under the social health insurance schemes was subject to an income ceiling. [1] In 1957, the public health insurance was extended with a social health insurance for the elderly with a low income. In 1968, the Exceptional Medical Expenses Act (AWBZ) is passed in Parliament, which represented a national insurance scheme covering the whole population for the high costs of long term care related to chronic physical and mental illness. In 1974, a new

proposal to change the health insurance act again was discussed in Parliament. But it would take more than thirty years before the plans were realized. Meanwhile, with a worsening economic crisis in the mid seventies, the government invested heavily in schemes to reduce insurance premiums for the elderly. On January 1 2006, a new Health Insurance Act (HIA) came into force in The Netherlands.

By virtue of this new Act, everyone who is legally living or working in the Netherlands is obliged in principle to take out a basic health insurance. The standard package, as determined by the government, includes General Practitioner costs, hospital care, midwifery costs and pharmacy costs. Health insurers have to accept everyone for basic health insurance whatever their age, gender or health. Conscientious objectors (those who on grounds of faith or philosophy of life do not want to take out insurance) and soldiers in active service are excluded. Children under the age of 18 years are also required to take out insurance but they do not have to pay premiums. They are included in their parents' policy free of charge. [2] Individuals can insure themselves for supplementary costs of care which is not included in the standard package, such as physiotherapy or dental care. The provisions and premiums of those insurances vary by insurer. The government has no control over supplementary insurance.

Households with an income below a certain level receive for the insurance premium for supplementary insurance in the form of a health care allowance from the government.

Under the 2006 Act, people are no longer automatically insured, but are obliged by law to purchase health insurance. Those who do not purchase a basic health insurance are automatically classified as 'uninsured'. This is an important difference from the scheme under the Sickness Fund Decree, which automatically covered each eligible person. The government uses penalties to keep the number of uninsured as low as possible for example, those who are uninsured are liable to pay a fine over the period of non-insurance, which can extend up to a maximum of five years, as well to pay any medical costs incurred during the uninsured period. Further refusal to take out insurance can be punished by the government compulsorily withholding earnings. [3]

Uninsured persons must be distinguished from defaulters. Defaulters are defined as subscribers who failed to pay their premium for a period of at least six months. In this situation, insurers, then have the legal right to stop the contractual arrangement. In order to avoid this situation, the government introduced a regulation in 2009 which gives insurers the right to enforce defaulters to pay premiums while maintaining their membership and preventing any switch to another health insurer, otherwise known as frivolous 'hopping'. Additionally, insurance funds agreed with the government that they will bear the financial risk over the first six months of defaulting after which period the government will assume this risk. The government also agreed a monitoring program to rapidly identify and track defaulters. Several penalties are used to compel them to pay their premium. [4]

It is undesirable to have civilians uninsured for several reasons. Firstly, the basis from the HIA is formed by the solidarity principle which states that everyone should contribute to the common facilities, regardless of how often he himself must rely upon. [5] If individuals do not take out basic health insurance this principle is undermined. Health insurers stand to lose income and the people who are insured have to pay a higher premium for their insurance.

Secondly, there may be effects on public health. Research shows that a lack of health insurance has a negative impact on access to medical services, quality of care and health status. [6-11] Even for short periods of lack of insurance ('churning') one already sees shifting in the usage of care, such as the postponement of care, insufficient usage –for instance of medication-, cancellation and a shift from regular care to emergency care. [12, 13] The quality of care for the uninsured lags behind in certain respects. In particular, the continuity of treatment and the quality of the relationship with medical professionals is reduced. [12, 13] There are also indications that differences in use of care and quality of care have an impact on health status. [14, 15] The lack of a health insurance increases mortality risk. In 2009, an estimated 44,789 deaths per year in the United States were associated with lack of health insurance. [16, 17]

Prior to the introduction of the HIA the issue of non-insurance was not high on the Dutch political agenda. Historically, the Netherlands has enjoyed a high rate of health insurance coverage. In 2005, only about 1.5% or the population did not have a health insurance. This percentage was however much higher among marginalized groups such as homeless people, addicted persons and long-term psychiatric patients. [18, 19] A review showed that between 1990 and 2006 the insurance rate of these groups in the four major cities in the Netherlands, Amsterdam, Rotterdam, The Hague and Utrecht, varied between 15% (residentially homeless) to 45% (night drifters). [20] The HIA of 2006 attempts to achieve universal coverage including these marginalised groups. Various provisions at national and municipality level have been taken to achieve this goal. [21-24]

> Care inclusion criteria for Public Mental Healthcare (PMHc)
> In Utrecht PMHc target group will get access to care under the following conditions:
> Persons of 18 years and older
> - who have problems in more than one aspect of life such as (imminent) homelessness, insufficient self-care, anti-social behaviour or serious debts,
> - who have psychiatric problems and/or are addicted, have cognitive problems and/or inadequate coping strategies
> - who display care-avoiding behaviour or are unable to find the way to social services
> - who need care that is not available in the standard care packages

In 2005, the municipality of Utrecht coordinated by the Municipal Health Service (MHS) started an intensive information campaign together with care providers and social relief services targeted at various marginalised groups. A collective health care insurance was taken out for the lowest income groups with a supplementary package with premium reduction. Persons without a permanent address were allowed to use the postal address of the municipal social service or care providers in order to register for health insurance. In order to avoid lack of health insurance and increasing individual debts because of the penalty system in place, the municipality of Utrecht deducts the monthly health insurance premium automatically from the social security benefit payment, provided the patient has given them permission to do so. The health care allowance may then be paid directly to the insurer. Additionally, compulsory budget management can be imposed on those individuals receiving social security benefit who are not able to organise their own lives, among them many Public Mental Health Care (PMHc) clients. By means of centralised applications, standardised indications, integral care and case management, Utrecht provides focused attention to get the PMHc target group insured and to keep them insured. [25, 26]

In order to monitor the situation of the PMHc target group Utrecht followed the insurance status of 3,168 persons over a period of 3.5 years, from July 2004 to January 2008. A further assessment was made on 1 January 2011. The objectives were to answer the following questions:

- Did the number of uninsured among the PMHc target group in Utrecht increase or decrease during the period July 1 2004 to January 1 2008?

- Are the differences in trends in uninsurance rate due to socio-demographic variables and the kind of health problem?
- How did the insurance rate develop after 2008?
- Can specific individual profiles be distinguished based on time patterns in insurance status?
- Is there a relationship between case management and insurance rate?

METHODS

Research Population

This research was set up as a cohort study, in which participants were followed both retrospectively and prospectively. The basic population for the cohort consisted of 3,168 persons registered with one or more institutions or services for PMHc in Utrecht during the period July 1 2004 to May 1 2006. These include homeless shelters, primary care services for the homeless, mobile outreach teams, day care centres for drug addicts and housing accommodation for socially vulnerable persons. (A definition of the PMHc target group is provided in the framed text above). A social medical doctor of the MHS handled the registration data so that privacy was protected.

Data Collection

At 14 points in time the insurance status was determined by consulting VECOZO (Safe Communication in Care), an Internet portal for information exchange between health care providers and insurance organizations (www.vecozo.nl). The portal allows access to the insurance data of people who had or have at any given time taken out a health care insurance with one of the associated care insurers. VECOZO was founded in 2002. In 2006, all health insurance organizations were using the services of VECOZO. The patients' insurance data remains available in VECOZO for two years. For the interrogation of the VECOZO database, the following search criteria were used: family name, initials, date of birth and gender. The first assessment took place in May 2006. Retrospectively the insurance status was also measured on July 1 2004, January 1 2005, January 1 2006 and March 1 2006. Further prospective measurements took place on September 1 2006, January 1 2007,

March 1 2007, May 1 2007, July 1 2007, September 1 2007, November 1 2007 and January 1 2008. A final assessment-was carried out in January 2011. Up to July 1 2007 checks were performed manually. There after, COV4U was used, a programme with which the insurance status of large groups of people can be determined automatically through different parameters (www.promeetec.nl). It was established whether a client was insured or not (VECOZO code: 'not insured' and 'insurance concluded'). Clients that could initially not be traced through VECOZO, but could be found at a later date, were given a 'not insured' status retrospectively.

Socio-demographic features, gender, date of birth and ethnicity, were obtained from the registratries of local institutions and those of the MHS Utrecht. In the Netherlands ethnicity is defined on the basis of country of birth. Clients are considered ethnic Dutch if they and both their parents were born in the Netherlands. For the co-variables homelessness and addiction problems, proxy-variables were used. Homelessness was determined from the address data in VECOZO at the start of the research. Persons for whom there was no known address and those with a P.O. Box number or the address of a homeless shelter were classified as homeless. The presence of addiction problems was ascertained based on whether a person's name occurred in the register of care and treatment of drug addicts and/or hostels for alcohol or drug addicts. Information on case management was derived from records of the MHS Utrecht in 2011.

Statistical Analysis

All statistical analysis was carried out by SPSS 19.0 for Windows. Generalized Estimating Equations (GEE) was used to analyse trends on a population level. GEE is a variation on Generalized Linear Models suited for repeated measuring of persons and for dichotomous outcome variables. Time expressed in the number of years lapsed since T0 and rounded off to 2 decimals, was included in the model as continuous variable. The data from the first 13 measurements were used for this purpose – T0 (July 2004) and T13 (January 2008). With Corrected Quasi-likelihood under Independence Model Criterion (QICC) the best fitting correlation structure was determined. The following options were tested: AR(1) ('auto regressive with lag 1'), exchangeable, independent and unstructured. The best fit was acquired with an exchangeable correlation structure. There were no missing observations. The logit function was chosen as it fitted the observed data best. Trends were determined for different sub populations by gender, age category, presence of addiction problems and homelessness. For each subpopulation a 95% confidence interval was computed for the odds ratio and interaction term. These analyses give insight into the dynamics at group level. In order to test changes in insurance status at an individual level, the 'proportion of change' was measured i.e. the proportion of people changing their insurance status. [27] At 4 timepoints: January 1 2005, 2006, 2007 and 2008, the 'proportion of increase' and the 'proportion of decrease' were calculated. The proportion of increase is the share of the entire cohort of both insured and uninsured persons, which changes from the status 'insured' to the status 'uninsured'. The proportion of decrease is the share of persons that changes its status of 'uninsured' to the status 'insured'. The trend in time was tested using GEE.

With the data obtained at the last measurement in January 2011, group differences were examined using Pearson chi-square test with post-hoc testing. Individual insurance profiles were drawn up based on the number and type of changes in insurance status and statistically tested.

RESULTS

Number and Demographics of a PMHc cohort

The basic population for the cohort consisted of 3,168 persons. Records with incomplete information on gender, date of birth, family name or initials were excluded (n=370). Besides 245 persons who died during the course of the research period (July 1 2004 to January 1 2011), the following were excluded: 33 persons that moved abroad, 137 persons illegally resident in the Netherlands, and 178 persons who did not feature in the data files of the insurers and of whose insurance status could not be determined (table 1). After these exclusions the cohort consisted of 2,205 persons.

Over three quarters of the cohort members were male (76.6%). The average age on January 1 2011 was 46.0 years (sd 12.0). Sixty-two percent were ethnic Dutch and 25.8% had ethnicity other than Dutch. The ethnicity of 12.1% of the clients was unknown. Of the cohort members 36.3% was defined as homeless at the start of the research and 23.5% suffered from severe addiction problems (table 2).

Table 1. Number of persons who are excluded according to the exclusion criteria (n=3, 168)

Exclusion criteria	Number of persons
Incomplete personal data	370
Illegal	137
Deceased	245
Moved abroad	33
Unknown in VECOZO	178
Total	953

Table 2. Individual insurance profiles PMHc cohort, January 2011

Variable	Prevalence (%)				
	A. Continuously insured	B. Newly un-insured	C. Newly insured	D. Off and on insured	TOTAL
	(n=1,212)	(n=132)	(n=408)	(n=453)	(n=2,205)
Gender					
Female	26.9	24.2	18.6	17.9	23.4
Male	73.1*	75.8	81.4*	82.1*	76.6
Age at 1.1.2011	47.7**	45.0	44.5	43.1	46.0
(year: average and SD)	(12.3)	(13.7)	(11.2)	(10.3)	(12.0)
Ethnicity					
Dutch	67.5 *	57.6	52.9 *	57.6 *	62.2
Other ethnicities	21.6 *	22.7	33.6 *	30.7 *	25.8
Unknown	10.9	19.7 *	13.5	11.7	12.1
Problems of addiction					
Yes	19.1*	12.1*	32.4*	30.9*	23.5
Not severe	80.9	87.9	67.6	69.1	76.5
Homeless					
Yes	29.9*	30.3	46.8*	45.9*	36.3
No	70.1	69.7	53.2	54.1	63.7
Case Manager					
Yes	33.8	19.7*	40.4*	33.3	36.3
No	66.2	80.3	59.6	66.7	65.9

* Pearson chi-square test with post-hoc testing based on adjusted residuals, p<.05.

** Anova with LSD post hoc test, p<.05.

Trend Analysis at Group Level

Figure 1a shows the progress in insurance status of 2.205 persons during the first research period from July 1 2004 to January 1 2008. The percentage of uninsured decreased from 27.4% in July 2004 to 12.4% in January 2008. The chances of being uninsured compared to the chances of being insured decreased annually by 0.718. A similar decrease was noted in men and women and across different age groups (table 3). Among the homeless, the percentage of uninsured decreased from 33.4% to 13.3% (Odds Ratio 0.715) and among addicts from 36.8% to 10.7% (OR 0.632). The odds ratio of the interaction term time*addiction was 0.946 (95% CI (0.914-0.980)). This indicates that the number of uninsured among addicts showed a stronger decline during the research period compared to non-addicted clients. Figure 1b depicts these trends graphically.

Table 3. Trends in being uninsured, odds ratio per year and interaction terms with 95% confidence interval (95% CI) according to gender, age group, severe addiction problems, and homelessness

	N	Trend * OR (95% CI)	Interaction term ** OR (95% CI)
Time (in years)	2205	**0.718 (0.685-0.752)**	
Gender			
Female	515	**0.714 (0.641-0.796)**	0.996 (0.883-1.123)
Male	1690	**0.717 (0.681-0.756)**	
Age 39 years or younger	1202	**0.726 (0.684-0.771)**	0.985 (0.955-1.016)
40 years or older	1003	**0.699 (0.647-0.755)**	
Addiction problems			
Yes	519	**0.632 (0.577-0.691)**	**0.946 (0.914-0.980)**
Not severe	1686	**0.753 (0.712-0.795)**	
Homeless			
No	1404	**0.710 (0.663-0.761)**	1.002 (0.972-1.032)
Yes	801	**0.715 (0.669-0.764)**	

* Odds ratio is determined for each subgroup (split file). Statistically significant odds ratios are in bold.

** Model tested with interaction term subgroup* time. Statistically significant odds ratios are in bold.

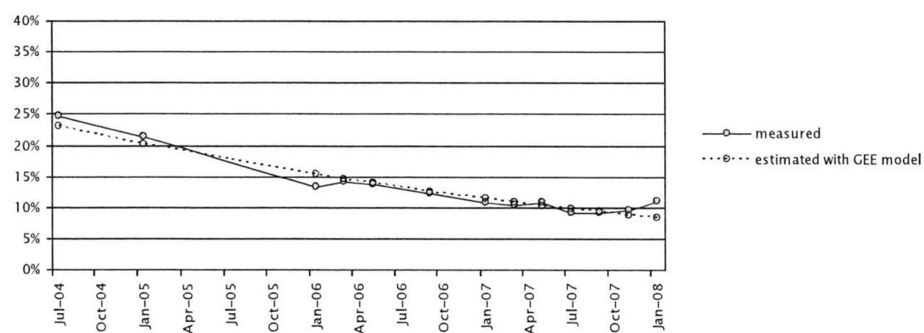

Figure 1a. Percentage of uninsured on 13 moments in the period July 2004-January 2008 in total cohort, measured and estimated with a GEE model.

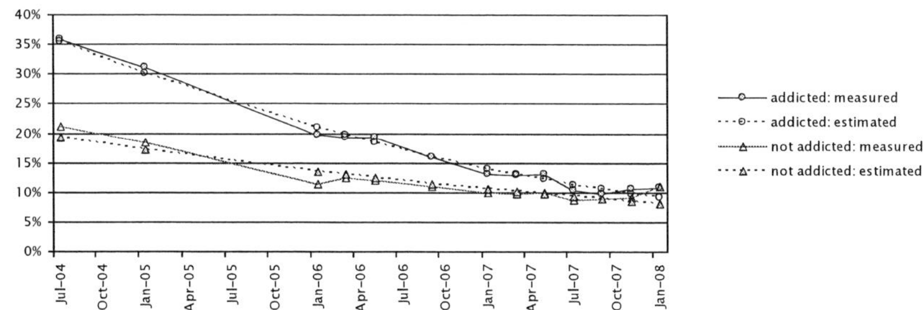

Figure 1b. Percentage of uninsured on 13 moments in the period July 2004-January 2008 in addicted and non-addicted groups, measured and estimated with a GEE model.

Insurance Status Switching at Individual Level

The decrease in the number of uninsured is the result of two processes:-uninsured persons who take out insurance,-and insured persons who become uninsured. Figure 2 shows switching of insurance status at four timepoints during the study. It illustrates that dynamics inside the PMHc cohort are greater than expected on the grounds of figure 1. Between January 1 2006 and January 1 2007, the percentage of uninsured in the cohort fell from 15.7% to 12.7% i.e. a difference of 3.0% (Figure 1). The proportion of change in the same period was 12.2%: 4.6% of the cohort members became uninsured (proportion of increase) and 7.6% became insured (proportion of decrease). One year earlier the dynamics were even stronger. Between January 1 2005 and January 1 2006 the proportion of increase was 14.6% and the proportion of decrease 6.1%.

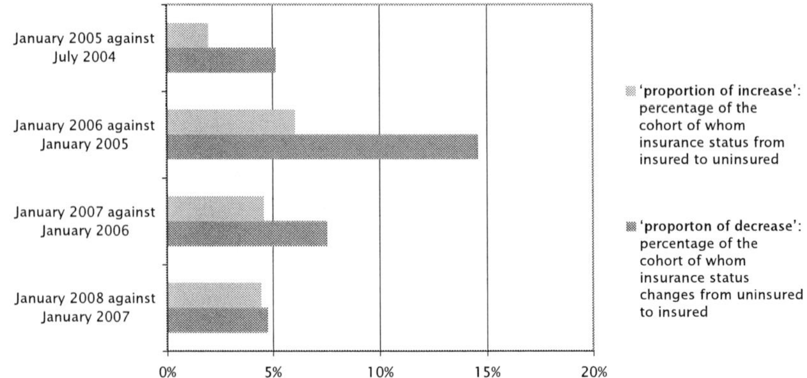

Figure 2. Percentage of PMHc cohort that switched insurance status, on four timepoints (N=2,205).

Trends in the proportion of increase and proportion of decrease are determined using GEE. Due to the fit of data, only the last three assessment timepoints have been used. The analyses show that since January 2005, the odds of changing from being insured to being uninsured decrease annually by 0.842 (95% CI (0.732, 0.969)), while the odds of going from uninsured to insured decreased by 0.531 (95% CI (0.472, 0.597)). As a result, January 1 2008 showed only a slightly positive balance: 4.4% of the cohort members became uninsured, in comparison with 4.8% who became insured.

Insurance Status January 2011

The stagnating trend observed in 2008, was reason for rechecking the insurance status of the cohort members three years later, in January 2011. The results are shown in table 4. Twelve percent of the cohort members were uninsured in January 2011. GEE analysis revealed no significant decrease since the last measurement in January 2008 (p=0.656). The percentage of uninsured is higher among clients younger than 40 years and non-Dutch clients. Clients with a case manager are less frequently uninsured.

Four groups can be distinguished based on their insurance behaviour:
- *Group A:* the "continuously insured". This is the largest group with 1,212 persons or 55.0% of the PMHc cohort, who were already insured before the new care system was introduced and continued to be so up to January 1 2011.

- *Group B:* the "newly uninsured". This is the smallest group with 132 persons or 6.0% of the PMHc cohort, who were insured before the new care system was introduced but became uninsured in the period thereafter and remained so until January 2011.
- *Group C:* the "newly insured". This group – 408 persons or 18.5% of the PMHc cohort – consists of uninsured who between July 1 2004 and January 1 2008 took out insurance and remained insured.
- *Group D:* the "off and on insured". This group – 453 persons or 20.5% of the PMHc cohort – switched insurance status more than once.

Table 2 shows the composition of the four groups. Group A, the continuously insured, is characterised by a higher number of women (26.9%), higher average age (47.7 years at January 1, 2011), lower percentage of non-Dutch clients (21.6%), fewer severe addiction problems (19.1%) and fewer homelessness (29.9%) than other groups.

Table 4. Percentage uninsured January 2011 (N=2,205)

Variable	%	N	p
Total	12.0	264	
Gender			
Male	12.5	211	.188
Female	10.3	53	
Age at 1.1.2011			
39 years of younger	15.3	107	.001
40 years or older	10.4	157	
Ethnicity			
Dutch	9.8	135	.000
Other ethnicities	13.9	79	
Unknown	18.8	50	
Problems of addiction			
Yes	13.1	68	.355
Not severe	11.6	196	
Homeless			
Yes	13.5	156	.102
No	11.1	108	
Personal case management			
Yes	9.0	68	.002
No	13.5	196	

Group B is characterised by a higher percentage of unknown ethnicity (19.7%), fewer addiction problems, and fewer clients receiving case management than on average. In groups C and D the proportion of women is lower (18.6% and 17.9% respectively), non-Dutch clients are more frequent than on average (33.6% and 30.7% respectively) and both the number of addicts (32.4% and 30.9% respectively) and homeless are higher (46.8% en 45.9% respectively) than on average. Group C has the highest percentage of clients with case management (40.4%).

DISCUSSION

This retrospective and prospective study describes the changes in health insurance status of a cohort of PMHc clients before and after the HIA came into force in January 2006. Instead of being insured automatically, civilians are obliged to purchase health insurance.The provision should prevent citizens from behaving themselves as 'free riders', but could raise barriers for certain excluded groups who have insufficient skills to meet their civil obligations. This could result in more homeless people and other PMHc target groups becoming and remaining uninsured.

The present study shows that overall, the number of the uninsured decreased in the PMHc group since the HIA was enacted. The percentage of the uninsured fell from 27.4% in July 2004 to 12.4% in January 2008. The provisions put in place by the municipality of Utrecht appear to have been effective. What is striking, however, is that the decreasing trend had already begun before the introduction of the HIA and that the decrease in uninsuredness was more pronounced among addicts.

In 2001 the Municipality of Utrecht had started the implementation of a comprehensive plan to provide structural accommodation to addicted homeless people in order to reduce the disruption and criminality that was associated with this group. They were offered living space and prolonged care in residential homes. Financing of these homes is made from the Exceptional Medical Expenses Act, which is linked to health insurance. In 2004, MHS encouraged PMHcare providers in Utrecht to seek funding through the Exceptional Medical Expenses Act. To qualify for the care, health insurance was necessary. [28] The policy to get the group of addicted homeless people off the streets and into support, may well have contributed to these findings.

The trend of falling numbers of uninsured clients observed between 2004 and 2008 has stopped. No significant decrease was found in the period 2008-2011. In January 2011, 12.0% of the cohort members were uninsured. The highest percentages of uninsured were found in the group under the age of 40 years and among non Dutch clients. This is comparable with the characteristics of uninsured clients in the general population. [29] However the number of uninsured in the general population is significantly lower than the PMHc group. In May 2010 only 0.8% of the Dutch population was uninsured and the numbers are still falling. [29] Our group of uninsured persons consists of a hard core group, which became uninsured after the introduction of the HIA and remained uninsured (6.0%) (Group B) and a group (D) of 'off and on' insured clients who oscillate between being insured and uninsured (20.5%). Group B is characterised by a higher percentage unknown ethnicity (19.7%), fewer addiction problems and fewer clients receiving case management than on average. It could either be a sign of a less problematic group or be a typical profile of care avoiders. Further investigation will be necessary to find out more about this group.

The group of 'off and on' insured client (group D) also includes defaulters, who with the information available to the study group were undistinguishable from uninsured client. Both categories fall under different regulations. However, due to the financial impediments and the actual deferment of insurance claims by the insurers, the difference between defaulter and uninsured is mostly semantic in real life. The group of off and on insured may also contain persons who are or have been detained in jail during the research period. As a consequence of their behaviour and lifestyle the PMHc group does come frequently in contact with the police. In 2008 half of new PMHc clients had in the preceding five years been in contact with police or judiciary. [30] This could be for public drinking or in limited cases more serious and frequent violations of the law which could lead to imprisonment. Detainees fall during their imprisonment under a regulation of the Ministry of Justice and their basic health insurance is suspended. As this is not recorded in VECOZO we can not quantify the impact on our results.

Following an earlier evaluation of the impact of the introduction of the HIA on the insurance status of PMHc clients in Utrecht 2008, we recommended more focussed and intensive case management to be put in place for both groups of uninsured. [31] The data from January 2011 show that clients with a personal case manager have a higher chance of becoming newly insured and less likely to become uninsured. The recommendations made earlier to focus and intensify case management appear to be effective.

This study has both strengths and limitations. The strong points are the length of time over which data were collected, the large number of participants and the diversity of the research group. The study included not only homeless people staying in shelters but also vulnerable groups in both recovery and prevention programmes. One limitation, however, is that a closed cohort was used. We determined the group at risk at one specific moment in time. It is possible that persons did not longer meet the criteria for PMHc target group after July 1 2006 and were thus incorrectly included in the cohort. As the problems faced by the PMHc group are severe, interrelated and persistent and the period of recovery is mostly long, we expect that the use of a closed cohort may only have resulted in some bias.

Another limitation of this study is the selection of clients is based on registration data. We cannot rule out that people made use of PMHc services without meeting the PMHc criteria. However we estimate these numbers to be small. The capacity of PMHc services is limited and those receiving care are necessarily selected where vacancies are given to those who really need care. Moreover, the services offered are not really attractive to people who do not belong to the target group. A further consequence of the use of registration data is that people who met the PMHc criteria but did not appeal for assistance, were not included in this study. This influences the generalising effect of the study.

Despite these limitations, our study provides important information regarding the uninsured who are in contact with social workers.

Being uninsured has a negative impact on the access, use and quality of care. A lack of health insurance is associated with increased risk of death. In the PMHc target group, where care avoidance is the rule rather than the exception, not having health care insurance can be quite a disadvantage. Another associated problem is that these people will see their debts increase which delays their recovery and may lead to relapse. In order to achieve a further reduction in the number of uninsured more measures will need to be taken. The Ministry of Health, Welfare and Sports came to the same conclusion, and advocates an active search based on file linking. [18] One must be aware that despite all measures there will always remain a group with a lack of insurance and due to the financial consequences, the focus should be on the defaulters. Locally, the best approach appears to be to focus on the group that runs the highest risk, however the hard core of uninsured PMHc members in Utrecht hardly deviates from the average PMHc member in respect of socio demographic features and problems. A broad approach, focused on the individual, seems to be the only option. In this regard, the integral approach of the case managers to take care of the insurance at the first interview, deserves to be developed further. Furthermore, MHS can regularly check the insurance status of PMHc-clients with an active file and give feedback to the case managers. If the approach is improved for those who enter and leave prison and for those who lose their benefits, this might yield great profits. It is essential that a prisoner has an allowance or work when he is released. Thus, importantly, social workers should cooperate in taking care of this target group in different fields.

REFERENCES

[1]   Vonk RAA. The long road to managed competition: *Sickness funds and the changes in the Dutch health insurance system,* 1941-2006. Amsterdam: Centre for the History of Health Insurance; 2010.

[2]   http://www.cvz.nl/verzekeringen/zvw.

[3]   Ministry of Health, Welfare and Sports (VWS). *The new care system in the Netherlands durability, solidarity, choice, quality, efficiency.* The Hague: Ministry of Health, Welfare and Sports; 2006.

[4]   Maarse H. *Private health insurance in the Netherlands.* Maastricht: University of Maastricht; 2009.

[5]   Ministry of Health, Welfare and Sports (VWS). Care insured. The introduction of the Health Insurance Act and potential uninsured: *report of a HEALTH-research.* The Hague: Ministry of Health, Welfare en Sports; 2005.

[6]   Eisert SL, Durfee MJ, Welsh A, Moore SL, Mehler PhS, Gabow PA. Changes in insurance status and access to care in an integrated safety net health care system. *J. Community Health.* 2009;34:122-8.

[7]   Skinner AC, Mayer ML. Effects of insurance status on children's access to speciality care: a systematic review of the literature. *BMC Health Serv. Res.* 2007;7:194.

[8]   Flores G, Vega LR. Barriers to health care access for Latino children: a review. *Fam. Med.* 1998;30(3):196-205.

[9]   McWilliams JM, Zaslavasky AM, Meara E, Ayanian JZ. Impact of Medicare coverage on basic clinical services for previously uninsured adults. *JANA* 2003;290(6):757-64.

[10]   Bachmann SS, Walter AW, Kuilan N, Lundgren LM. Implications of Medicaid coverage in a program for Latino substance users. *Eval. Program Plann.* 2008;31(1)74-82.

[11] Jeffrey AE, Newacheck PW. Role of insurance of children with special health care needs: a synthesis of the evidence. *Pediatrics* 2006; 118 (4): 1027-38.

[12] Summer L, C Mann. Instability of public health insurance coverage for children and their families: causes, consequences and remedies. Georgetown University Health Policy Institute. *The Common Wealth Fund,* 2006.

[13] Hoffman C, Schoen C, Rowland D, Davis K. Gaps in health coverage among working-age Americans and the consequences. *J. Health Care Poor Underserved* 2001;12(3):272-89.

[14] Hadley J. Insurance coverage, medical care use, and short-term health changes following an unintentional injury or the onset of a chronic condition. *JAMA* 2007; 297(10):1073-84.

[15] van den Born BJ, Koopmans RP, Groeneveld JO, van Montfrans GA. Ethnic disparities in the incidence, presentation and complications of malignant hypertension. *J. Hypertens* 2006; 24(11):2299-304.

[16] Morrison DS: Homelessness as an independent risk factor for mortality: results from a retrospective cohort study. *Intern. J. Epidemiol.* 2009;38:877-883.

[17] Wilper AP, Woolhandler S, Lasser KE, McCormick D, Bor DH, Himmelstein DU. Health insurance and mortality in US adults. *Am. J. Public Health.* 2009;99:1-7.

[18] Ministry of Health, Welfare and Sports (VWS).. *Verzekerdenmonitor* 2008. The Hague: Ministry of Health, Welfare and Sports;2008.

[19] Statistic Netherlands.. Forse toename wanbetalers, lichte afname onverzekerden in 2007. *CBS Persbericht PB06-033.* Voorburg/Heerlen: Centraal Bureau voor de Statistiek; 13 mei 2008.

[20] Rensen P. Dakloos en onverzekerd in de grote stad. *Een onderzoek naar de gevolgen van de invoering van de nieuwe zorgverzekeringswet voor daklozen in de vier grote steden.* Utrecht: Trimbos Instituut; 2007.

[21] Landelijke Vereniging van Thuislozen. Onderzoeks- en voorlichtingscampagne nieuwe zorgstelsel, fase 2. Amsterdam: LVT; 2006.

[22] Smit R. Zorgverzekeringswet: Zorgen voor anderen. *Gezondschrift* 2006; 16(3)3.

[23] Verkleij, H. Onverzekerd maakt onbemind. *TSG,* 2006; 84:257-9.

[24] van Bergen A, Smit R, van de Meulen R. Onverzekerd in Utrecht. Omvang en kenmerken van onverzekerden tegen ziektekosten in Utrecht. Analyse van CBS gegevens. *Utrecht: GG&GD Utrecht;* 2007.

[25]   http://www.utrecht.nl/smartsite.dws?id=32936.

[26]   Dutch Government Four Major Cities. *Strategy plan for Social relief.* The Hague: 7 february 2006.

[27]   Twisk JWR. Applied longitudinal data analysis for epidemiology. *A practical guide.* 4th ed. Cambridge: Cambridge University Press; 2007.

[28]   Mensink C, Meertens V, Wolf J, Smit R. Indicatiestelling bij sociaal kwetsbare mensen in Utrecht. *Gegevensanalyse van AWBZ-indicatieaanvragen* 2004. Uitgeverij SWP, Amsterdam, 2006.

[29]   Statistic Netherlands. Tien procent minder onverzekerden tegen ziektekosten in 2010 *CBS Persbericht PB11*-023. Voorburg/Heerlen: Centraal Bureau voor de Statistiek, 29 maart 2011.

[30]   van Bergen A, Smit RBJ, Reinking D, Muis L, van der Leer M, Kolen M, Oepkes N, Vleems R, van der Meer E, van Doeveren Y. Zorg voor sociaal kwetsbaren. *VMU rapport. Gemeente Utrecht*, Maart 2010.

[31]   van Bergen A, Smit RBJ, van Ameijden EJC. Veranderingen in verzekeringsstatus van een cohort Utrechtse Openbare Geestelijke Gezondheidszorg cliënten in de periode 2004-2008. *TSG* 2010;2:89-96.

In: Health Insurance   ISBN: 978-1-62081-050-7
Editors: E. Abrahamsen et al.   © 2012 Nova Science Publishers, Inc.

Chapter 3

ASSESSING THE EFFICIENCY OF HOSPITALS IN BOTSWANA: AN APPLICATION OF THE PABÓN LASSO TECHNIQUE

Justice Nonvignon[1,], Naomi Tlotlego[2],
Eyob Zere Asbu[3], Eugene Appiah Nyarko[4],
Joses Muthuri Kirigia[5] and Luis Gomes Sambo[5]*
[1]University of Ghana, School of Public Health, Legon, Ghana
[2]University of Botswana, Economics Department,
Gaborone, Botswana
[3] World Health Organization Regional Office for Africa,
Inter-country Support Team for East and Southern Africa,
Harare, Zimbabwe
[4]World Health Organization, Botswana Country Office,
Gaborone, Botswana
[5]World Health Organization Regional Office for Africa,
Brazzaville, Congo

ABSTRACT

The health system in sub-Saharan Africa faces a number of
challenges, including weak health systems structures. The ramifications

---

[*] Email: jnonvignon@ug.edu.gh.

of inefficiencies in the management of resources could jeopardise the development of health infrastructure and the coverage of health care, especially among the poor and underprevillaged. Consequently, efficient allocation and management of scarce resources could improve the health systems in the region. The 2010 World Health Report places much emphasis on the invaluable role that efficiency palys in achieving universal coverage. The aim of this chapter was to conduct an exploratory assessment of the performance of non-referral hospitals in Botswana for the period 2006 to 2008 using the Pabón Lasso technique. The results show that during each year in the study period, less than half of the hospitals operated efficiently while more than half operated with excess bed capacity. The findings of the study imply that rather than expanding hospital sizes by increasing the number of beds, there could be an expansion in the health services provided by hospitals. This provides an opportunity to improve maternal and child health services and accelerate progress towards the health-related Millennium Development Goal targets while moving the country towards universal coverage of health services.

Keywords: Health systems structures; hospital efficiency; Pabón Lasso technique; excess bed capacity; Botswana.

INTRODUCTION

Generaly, the health system in sub-Saharan African countries faces a number of challenges – a huge and growing burden of diseases such as HIV/AIDS, malaria and tuberculosis; dual burden of diseases related to the demographic and epidemiological transition; inadequate human, financial and other resources, and weak health systems structures. In recent years, however, the health sector has been receiving an increasing proportion of government budgetary allocations and donor support. Of concern to stakeholders in the health sector has been whether or not the sector makes optimal use of the resources committed to it given that major health indicators are not improving and the rate of progress to achieve the health-related Millennium Development Goals (MDGs) is slow. Under-five and maternal mortality in the region remain high at 145 per 1,000 live births and 900 per 100,000 live births respectively; healthy life expectancy at birth remains low at below 50 years [1].

Efficient allocation and management of resources could go a long way to improve health systems all over the world and sub-Sahara Africa in particular. It is for this reason that the 2010 World Health Report [2] places much emphasis on the invaluable role that efficiency palys in achieving universal coverage. While it is important to mobilize enough resources to cater for the health needs of a population, especially the poor and vulnerable, it is equally important that attention be given to the health outcomes that these resources produce.

The 2010 World Health Report presents some more general reasons why inefficiencies may exist in health facilities. Three out of the ten suggested reasons for inefficiency were related to the use of medicines and touched on issues concerning underuse of generics and higher than neccesary medicine prices, use of substandard and counterfiet medicine, inapropriate and ineffective medicine use. other sources of inefficiency include overuse or supply of equipments, investigations and procedures, inappropriate or costly staff mix, inappropriate hospital admissions and length of stay etc. [2].

The ramifications of inefficiencies in the management of health system resources can not be underestimated. On a larger scale, this could jeopardise the development of health infrastructure and the coverage of health care, especially among the poor and underprevillaged. Low income countries could save up to 12-24% of their total health expenditure by improving workforce or hospital efficiency [2] . This implies that low-income countries (whose health resources are usually scarce) could still free 12-24% of annual health expenditure under relatively efficient conditions which could be used to expand health coverage.

In addition to the above mentioned problem, inefficiencies could also lead to a compromise of the quality of services provided at various health facilities. Services that could be provided at lower costs are actually provided at higher costs while those that could be improved at the existing costs are left to suffer due to inefficiencies. Such situations mostly occur in public health facilities in developing countries where the majority of the pouplation seek care from. This could have negative impacts on the health of the population as a whole, if efforts are not put in place to rectify it.

As is the case in other sub-Saharan African countries, hospitals in Botswana consume the lion's share of health sector resources [3-4]. Worldwide, studies on the efficiency of health facilities have made extensive use of data Envelopement Analysis (DEA) technique [3, 5-8]. However, studies employing simpler methods like the Pabón Lasso technique also exist [9-10]. The objective of this study is to assess the performance of non-referral hospitals in Botswana. Specifically, the study seeks to explore capacity utilization of hospitals in Botswana using the Pabón Lasso technique and propose recommendations that are relevant for management decision making.

COUNTRY PROFILE

Botswana has a population of 1.921 million and with 2008 gross national income (GNI) per capita of $13,204 (2008 PPP), the country is categorized as a middle income country [11-13]. The country generaly has better development indicators compared to the average for Africa as shown by human development index of 0.593 (2005) and 0.633 (2010) compared to Africa's average of 0.366 (2007) and 0.389 (2010) (UNDP, 2010). In a recent report by the United Nations, Botswana was identified as having achieved the third highest growth rate in GNI per capita over the past three decades (behind China and South Korea), recording ninefold increase in per capita income between 1970 and 2010 [11].

With respect to commitment of resources to health, Botswana's total health expenditure per capita for 2008 stood at US$392.50 as against US$101.80 for the African region, while government expenditure on health as a percentage of total health expenditure of 74.3% is higher than the average for the region (Table 1). Also, the per capita total health expenditure at average exchange rate and per capita government health expenditure at average exchange rate are more than three times higher than the average for the African region. The density of health personnel such as physicians, nursing and midwifery staff and dentists in Botswana are all better than the average for Africa while the number of hospital beds per 10,000 population is also more than twice the African average (Table 1).

Statistics on the health-related millennium development goals indicates that the under-five mortality per 1,000 live births is 40 relative to a 145 average of the African region. Maternal mortality ratio (per 100,000 live births) is 380 which is lower in comparison to the african average of 900. Malaria mortality rate per 100,000 population stands at a low of 2 while the average of the african region is estimated to be 104. Access to improved drinking water sources and improved sanitation in Botwana is estimated to be 96% and 47% respectively and this still shows better conditions than the African average of 59% and 33% respectively [3].

Other important global health indicators show that Botwana has a life expectancy at birth of 56 years which is higher than the African average of 52 years. Similarly healthy life expectancy at birth in Botswana is given to be 49 years.

Table 1. MDG, health and National Health Accounts indicators

Indicator	Botswana	African Region
Under-5 mortality rate (probability of dying by age 5 per 1,000 live births	40	145
Maternal mortality ratio (per 100,000 live births)	380	900
Prevalence of HIV among adults aged >=15 years per 100,000 population	22757	4735
Malaria mortality rate per 100,000 population	2	104
Access to improved drinking-water sources (percent)	96	59
Access to improved sanitation (percent)	47	33
Life expectancy at birth in years	56	52
Healthy life expectancy (HALE) at birth (years)	49	45
Neonatal mortality rate (per 1,000 live births)	46	40
Infant mortality rate (probability of dying between birth and age 1 per 1,000 live births)	32	88
Adult mortality rate (probability of dying between 15 and 60 years per 1,000 population)	514	401
HIV/AIDS -specific mortality rate (per 100,000 population)	585	198
Malaria -specific mortality rate (per 100,000 population)	2	104
TB among HIV-negative people (per 100,000 population)	37	45
TB among HIV-positive people (per 100,000 population)	156.5	47.6
Prevalence of HIV among adults aged >15 years (per 100,000 population)	22757	4735
Physicians - Density (per 10,000 population)	4	2
Nursing and midwifery personnel (per 10,000 population)	27	11
Dentistry personnel (per 10,000 population)	<1	1
Hospital beds (per 10,000 population)	24	10
Health expenditure (2008)		
Total expenditure on health as percent of Gross domestic product	5.6	5.7
General government expenditure on health as percent of total expenditure on health	74.3	50.5
Private expenditure on health as percent of total expenditure on health	25.7	49.5
Per capita total expenditure on health at average exchange rate (US$)	392.5	101.8
Per capita government expenditure on health at average exchange rate (US$)	291.5	59.8

Source: Data from WHO, 2009.

The probability of dying between birth and the age of one per 1,000 live births (infant mortality rate) and adult mortality rate (the probability of dying between 15 and 60 years per 1,000 population) are given to be 32 and 514 respectively, relative to the African region average of 88 and 401 respectively. While HIV prevalence among adults above 15 years stands at 22.7%, HIV/AIDS specific mortality rate per 100,000 population is given to be 585. These present much worse statistics compared to the African region's average where prevalence of HIV among adults above the age of 15 is 4.7% and HIV/AIDS specific mortality rate per 100,000 population is 198. Moreover, while TB among HIV-positive people (per 100,000 population) is at a high of 156.5 in Botwana, it is estimated to be 47.6 in the African region (Table 1).

Table 1 also shows that Botwana has a physician density of 4 per 10,000 population relative to the African region average of 2. The country also has nursing and midwifery personnel of 27 per 10,000 population compared to 11 for the African region. Also, dentistry personnel in Botwana is less than 1 per 10,000 population relative to 1 dentistry personnel per 10,000 population for the African region.Again there are 24 hospital beds per 10,000 population in Botwana while the average for the entire African region is estimated to be 10 hospital beds per 10,000 population.

The above imply that Botswana commits more resources to health than the average for Africa. However, basic health indicators do not seem commensurate with such commitments in resources. As can be seen in Table 1, adult mortality rate for 2008, HIV-specific mortality, incidence and prevalence of tuberculosis among HIV-positive people are all higher than the average for the African region and prevalence of HIV among adults is almost five times higher than the average for the region. Gross national income (or gross domestic product) rank minus human development index (HDI) rank is a measure of the efficiency with which a country's resources are translated into welfare of the population. Using the GDP per capita rank minus HDI rank, Botswana obtained -70 for 2005 and -38 for 2008 [11]. This implies that on the macro level, there is gross inefficiency in translating resources into welfare in Botswana.

METHODS

Study Sample

All non-referral hospitals were surveyed. However, the study made use of a sample of 21 non-referral hospitals for which complete data were obtained.

Analytical Framework

The efficiency of hospitals can be measured by the use of capacity utilization ratios or by frontier techniques. Ratio analysis makes use of different key ratios such as cost per delivery or bed occupancy rate. The main advantages of this technique are the ease of use and interpretation, but there are also shortcomings, which include the requirement for identical measurement units and the use of single input and single output. The latter makes comparison between different decision making units (hospitals in this case) difficult since one hospital might be better off in, for instance, cost per in-patient day compared to another which might be better-off in cost per delivery for example. Ratio analysis requires specifying *a priori* weight and or a standardizing measurement to get an overall indicator. The commonly used ratios in analysing hospitals are discussed below.

a)   Average length of stay (ALS)

The average length of stay for a hospital is a measure of the average number of days that patients stayed in the hospitals for a given period. It is calculated using the formula:

$$ALS = \frac{Inpatient\ days}{admissions} \tag{1}$$

Using this measure, for a homogenous group of hospitals, those with lower average length of stay are considered as performing better than those with higher average length of stay. In Botswana, the ALS for health facilities is 6.4 days [14]. From the above formula, total inpatient days for a hospital can be calculated as the average length of stay multiplied by the total admissions.

b)   Bed occupancy rate (BOR)

This ratio measures how a hospital makes use of available beds. The measure gives an indication of the percentage of beds that are occupied by in-patients during a period of time. The following formula is used to calculate BOR:

$$BOR = \frac{inpatient\ days}{bed\ days} \times 100$$

(2)

Bed days in the formula above is calculated as the total number of beds multiplied by the number of days that the bed is available i.e. out of 365. The ideal BOR for hospitals to operate efficiently is 85-90 percent [15].

c)   Bed turnover ratio (BTR)

This ratio measures the productivity of the hospital bed during a period of time, usually one year and is computed as follows:

$$BTR = \frac{Total\ admissions}{number\ of\ beds}$$

(3)

The BTR is expected to be higher in acute care hospitals compared to chronic care hospitals [16].

d)   Turnover interval (TI)

Also known as the substitution interval, the turnover interval measures the average period during which hospital beds are left unoccupied between successive patients, i.e. between one discharge and the next admission. It is calculated as:

$$TI = \frac{365}{BTR} - ALS$$

(4)

The ideal turnover interval is 1-3 days [16].

The Pabón Lasso Technique

Pabón Lasso [17] developed a technique to analyze the performance of hospitals using the first three ratios i.e. bed turnover rate, bed occupancy rate and average length of stay. The method makes use of a graph with four Regions, which has bed occupancy rate plotted on the horizontal axis as against the turnover ratio on the vertical axis. On this graph, the inverse of the slope of the line drawn to link the origin to any point represents the average length of stay of the given observation.

From Figure 1, Region I is characterized by low turnover rate accompanied by low occupancy. A hospital in such a situation has excess bed supply resulting from either less need for hospitalization or low demand or utilization of services and cannot be said to perform well. The demand for services could also be influenced by the size of the catchment population or perceived quality of services.

In Region II, though the hospital has high BTR, it has low occupancy, implying excess bed capacity. The high BTR means that patients are admitted and discharged quickly, as is the case of deliveries. The opposite holds for a hospital in Region IV, which has high bed occupancy and low turnover. Thus, these hospitals can in no way be judged as performing well.

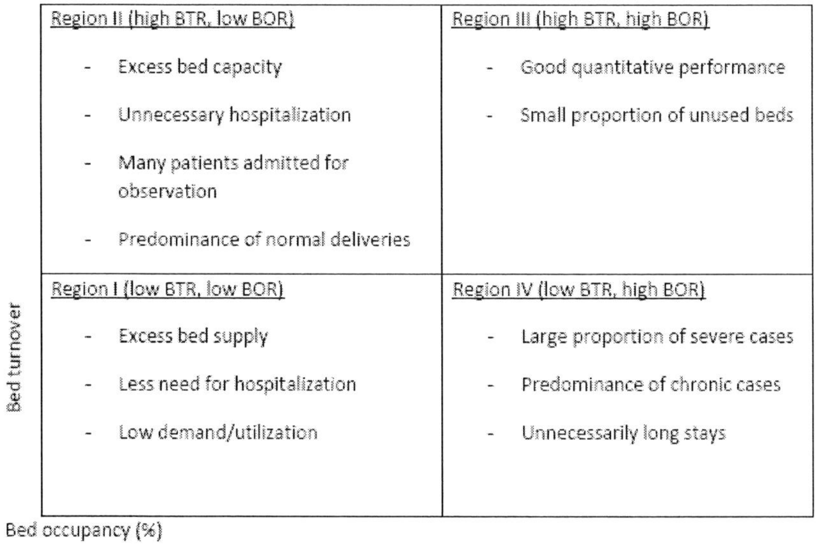

Region II (high BTR, low BOR)	Region III (high BTR, high BOR)
- Excess bed capacity - Unnecessary hospitalization - Many patients admitted for observation - Predominance of normal deliveries	- Good quantitative performance - Small proportion of unused beds
Region I (low BTR, low BOR)	Region IV (low BTR, high BOR)
- Excess bed supply - Less need for hospitalization - Low demand/utilization	- Large proportion of severe cases - Predominance of chronic cases - Unnecessarily long stays

Bed turnover (vertical axis) — Bed occupancy (%) (horizontal axis)

Figure 1. The Pabón Lasso Diagram.

However, a hospital in Region III has both high BTR and high occupancy. This implies that the hospital has a small proportion of unused beds, thus performing well i.e. making good use of all available beds.

Data

Data were collected on the inputs (i.e. number of clinical beds, number of admissions) and outputs (i.e. inpatient days) of each hospital in the sample for the period 2006 to 2008 using WHO/AFRO hospital efficiency questionnaire.

Data Analysis

Capacity utilization ratios for hospitals were computed using Microsoft Excel and STATA10 software.

RESULTS

Descriptive Statistics

Seventy-six percent (76%) of the hospitals analyzed were public hospitals, 10% were mission hospitals and the remaining 14% were private hospitals. Also, 76% of the hospitals were located in rural areas with the remaining 24% in urban areas. Table 2 shows the mean values of input and output variables for the hospitals in the sample.

Table 2 shows that the number of clinical beds changes over the study period, with mean of 97.5 beds in 2006 and increasing to 113 beds in 2008, ranging from 20 to 350 beds in 2006, 23 to 350 in 2007 and 23 to 350 beds in 2008. The mean number of admissions falls marginally from 3,556 in 2006 to 3,510.5 in 2007 but rises to 3,686 in 2008. The mean number of inpatient days follows the same trend.

Table 3 presents a summary of the capacity utilization indicators for the study period. The table shows that the mean average length of stay (ALS) of hospitals in Botswana fell marginally to 4.5 days in 2007 compared to 4.7 days in 2006 but increased to 4.9 days in 2008. Table 3 also shows a decline in the mean values for bed turnover ratio and bed occupancy rates between 2006 and 2008.

Table 2. Summary statistics for inputs and output, 2006 – 2008

Variable	2006 Mean	Std. Dev.	2007 Mean	Std. Dev.	2008 Mean	Std. Dev.
Clinical beds	97.5	75.6	98.4	75.3	113	98.6
Admissions	3,556.1	2,276.9	3,510.5	2,268.3	3,686	2,216.8
Inpatient days	17,570.7	13,012.9	16,669.4	11,711.0	18,836.4	12,564.7

Table 3. Mean capacity utilization ratios, 2006 – 2008

Variable	2006 Mean	Std. dev.	2007 Mean	Std. dev.	2008 Mean	Std. dev.
Average length of stay (days)	4.7	1.1	4.5	1.2	4.9	1.4
Bed turnover ratio	41.6	21.7	40.2	20.3	39.5	21.5
Bed occupancy rate (%)	53.8	30.2	50.3	30.3	53.7	36.5
Turnover interval (days)	7	8.1	8	9.9	9.8	17.3

The turnover interval increases from 7 days in 2006 to 8 days in 2007 and then rises again to 9.8 days in 2008.

The capacity utilization ratios of hospitals are presented in Table 4. The Pabón Lasso diagrams were used to analyze the annual performance of hospitals by their capacity utilization. In plotting the Pabón Lasso diagrams, one observation – i.e. Bobonong hospital – was dropped because it reported bed occupancy rates of 115.6% in 2006, 133.8% in 2007 and 171.2% in 2008. These values were considered as outliers. An Average turnover interval of 7 days or more over the three years period indicates that most of the beds remained unoccupied for a long period. This is consistent with the bed occupancy rates of around 50%.

The Pabón Lasso diagrams for 2006, 2007 and 2008 are presented in Figure 2, Figure 3 and Figure 4 respectively.

Table 4. Capacity utilization ratios for individual hospitals, 2006 - 2008

Hospital ID	Name	2006				2007				2008			
		ALS	BTR	BOR	TI	ALS	BTR	BOR	TI	ALS	BTR	BOR	TI
1	Rakops	6.00	35.95	59.09	4.15	6.00	36.03	59.22	4.13	6.00	39.72	65.29	3.19
2	Masunga	3.89	29.58	31.57	8.44	3.41	27.96	26.13	9.64	3.56	29.89	29.15	8.65
3	Mmadinare	3.09	24.35	20.58	11.91	1.76	23.47	11.30	13.79	1.44	25.47	10.07	12.89
4	Bobonong	5.55	76.03	115.61	-0.75	6.58	74.21	133.78	-1.66	7.66	81.58	171.20	-3.19
5	Palapye	5.00	70.38	96.41	0.19	4.33	70.40	83.52	0.85	4.00	72.52	79.47	1.03
6	Letlhakane	4.21	92.48	106.79	-0.27	3.78	69.32	71.80	1.48	5.01	67.12	92.21	0.42
7	Sefhare	4.22	49.00	56.68	3.23	3.78	42.82	44.35	4.74	4.83	34.90	46.17	5.63
8	Thebephatswa	4.00	8.87	9.72	37.15	4.00	7.33	8.03	45.82	4.00	4.26	4.67	81.66
9	Gweta	4.28	24.54	28.76	10.59	3.75	18.92	19.42	15.55	6.02	18.70	30.86	13.49
10	Kanye	8.03	37.80	83.15	1.63	6.73	32.71	60.28	4.43	6.48	33.48	59.45	4.42
11	Orapa	5.04	23.87	32.99	10.25	6.01	22.82	37.60	9.98	5.62	23.35	35.92	10.02
12	Maun	4.84	29.32	38.86	7.61	4.85	29.56	39.26	7.50	6.73	17.40	32.10	14.24
13	Phikwe	4.25	70.71	82.33	0.91	3.92	70.32	75.52	1.27	4.33	68.63	81.42	0.99
14	Scottish	4.31	35.75	42.25	5.90	4.25	44.01	51.29	4.04	4.77	20.93	27.35	12.67
15	Sekgoma	4.80	22.56	29.67	11.38	5.30	17.49	25.40	15.56	6.25	18.41	31.52	13.58
16	Athlone	5.61	25.20	38.71	8.88	4.85	27.40	36.43	8.47	4.21	30.81	35.56	7.63
17	Mahalapye	4.43	64.01	77.74	1.27	4.44	69.93	85.09	0.78	6.06	54.11	89.87	0.68
18	Delta	3.00	34.00	27.95	7.74	3.00	40.09	32.95	6.11	3.00	64.22	52.78	2.68
19	Jwaneng	3.86	27.29	28.85	9.52	4.32	26.36	31.17	9.53	4.05	28.10	31.21	8.93
20	Bamalete	5.10	52.78	73.75	1.82	5.20	54.73	77.98	1.47	4.70	51.44	66.24	2.40
21	Deborah	4.61	38.06	48.11	4.98	4.45	37.52	45.77	5.28	4.54	43.75	54.39	3.80

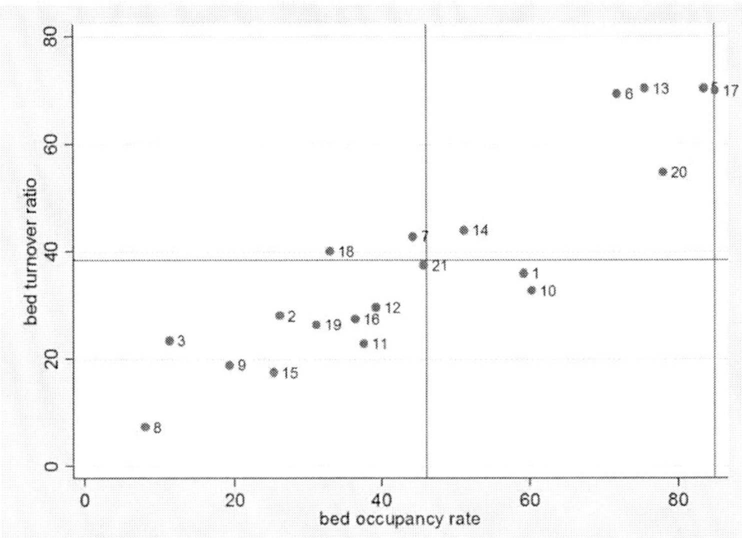

Figure 2. Pabón Lasso diagram, 2006.

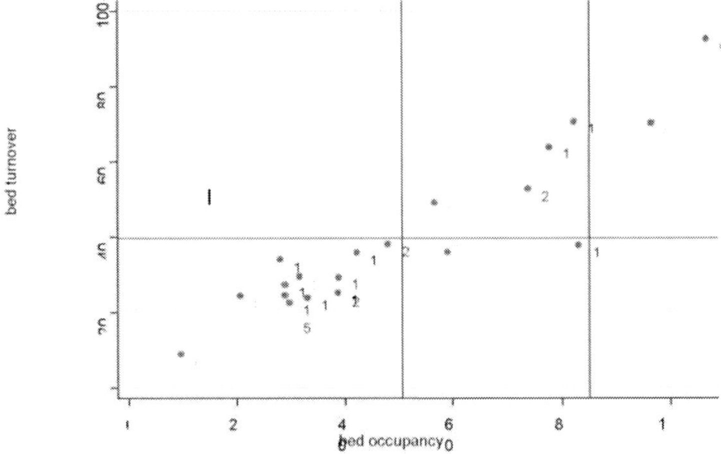

Figure 3. Pabón Lasso diagram, 2007.

During the analysis, two types of scenarios were done, varying the mean bed occupancy in each case. In the first case, the mean bed turnover ratio and bed occupancy rate for the hospitals in the sample was used as a benchmark to compare the performance of each hospital.

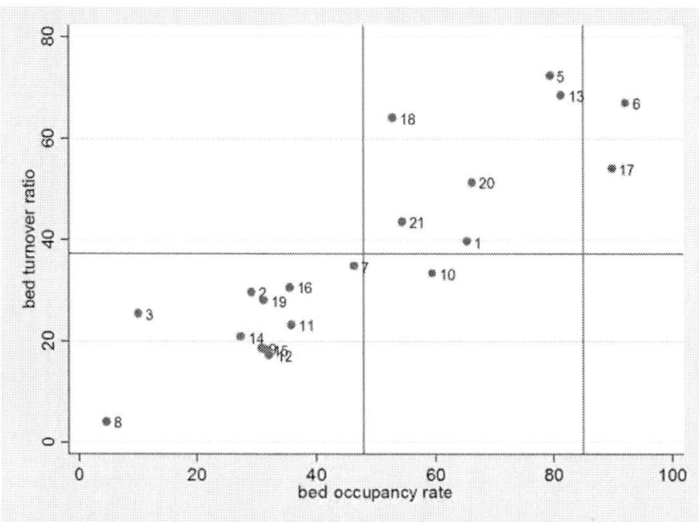

Figure 4. Pabón Lasso diagram, 2008.

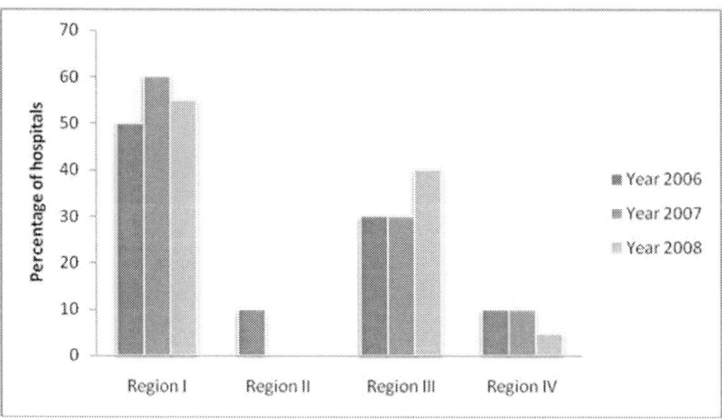

Figure 5. Distribution of hospitals on the Pabón Lasso diagram using sample mean occupancy.

Using this benchmark, the numbers of hospitals which fall within Region I (i.e. the bottom left region of the graph) are 10, 12 and 11, representing 50%, 60% and 55% for 2006, 2007 and 2008 respectively. This region represents poor performance or inefficiency. In contrast, 6, 6 and 8 hospitals representing 30%, 30% and 40% for 2006, 2007 and 2008 respectively fall within Region

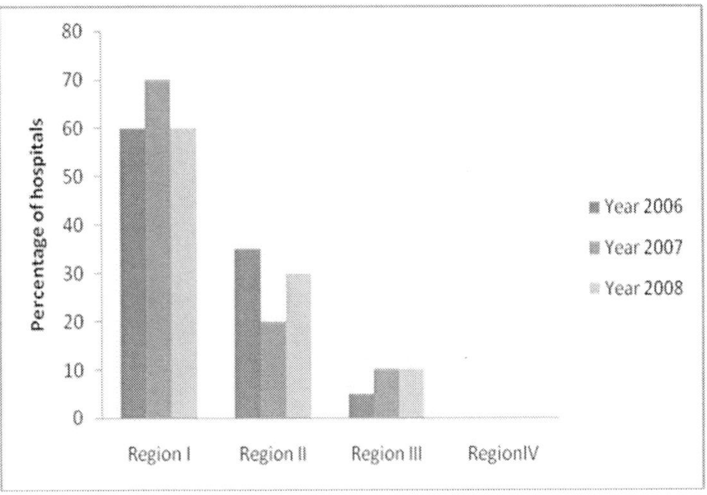

Figure 6. Distribution of hospitals on the Pabón Lasso diagram using 85 percent occupancy.

III which represents good quantitative performance. Figure 5 presents a first scenario, which shows the percentages of hospitals which fall within the various Regions using the sample mean occupancy.

The second scenario employs the mean bed turnover of the sample and bed occupancy of 85% accepted for international standards. Using this as the benchmark, the number of hospitals in the inefficient Region (i.e. Region I) increases to 12, 14, and 12, representing 60%, 70% and 60% of hospitals for 2006, 2007 and 2008 respectively. This reduces the efficient hospitals to 1, 2 and 2 representing 5%, 10% and 10% for 2006, 2007 and 2008 respectively. Figure 6 shows the percentages of hospitals which fall within the various Regions under the second scenario.

The study finds that even when the mean turnover and occupancy of the sample of hospitals are used as benchmark, 50%, 60% and 55% of the hospitals operate in the lower left Region of the Pabón Lasso diagram in 2006, 2007 and 2008 respectively, indicating poor performance. This result is consistent with the finding that close to 50% of primary level hospitals in Malawi operate in the lower left Region of the Pabón Lasso diagram [16]. This could be due to one factor or a combination of factors such as excess bed supply, less need for hospitalization or low demand/utilization, which might not necessarily imply excess capacity relative to need as this study did not assess the need for services.

Though the study did not seek to examine which of the above factors is responsible for the poor performance, the underlying issue is that during the period 2006 and 2008, between 30% and 40% of the hospitals were efficient in each year as they had small proportion of unused beds while between 50% to 60% were inefficient as they had excess bed supply. This finding is corroborated by Tlotlego et al [3] who find that 76%, 76% and 62% of the same sample of hospitals used in this study were inefficient in 2006, 2007 and 2008 respectively using data envelopment analysis.

Bed occupancy rates reflect the ability of a hospital to provide safe and efficient care. It is widely accepted that BORs of more than 85% indicate overcrowding and a greater likelihood of nosocomial infections [18]. However, in the case of hospitals in Botswana, there is gross underutilization of hospital beds, which implies the underutilization of other complementary inputs such as human resources, physical space and others on the assumption that staffing and budget levels of hospitals have a positive correlation with the number of beds in a hospital.

All other things constant, we would expect the rate of nosocomial infections to be negligible in this sample of non-referral hospitals in Botswana, given that beds remain unoccupied for a long period of time after a patient is discharged (high turnover intervals of more than 7 days).

The fact that the bed density in Botswana is only 1 per 1,000 population may indicate that there is a significant unmet need for hospital beds. However, the paradox of low bed occupancy rates in the face of low bed density may imply that there are both supply and demand-side factors that need to be considered before making the conclusion that excess bed-supply exists. On the supply side, factors such as distance to facility, issues related to responsiveness (client satisfaction) of the hospital system and perceived quality of care are, presence of (un)official user fees are some of the factors that could discourage utilization of hospital inpatient services. Equally important are demand-side factors, which may include care-seeking behaviour of the population, the opportunity cost of care seeking, etc. It is therefore important to investigate factors that are responsible for the low utilization of hospital inpatient services and design evidence-based interventions to address the problem and utilize the existing hospital beds to an acceptable level. Without such measures, such critically low capacity utilization may lead to inefficiency and wastage of resources that could have been used otherwise in other health-enhancing activities.

CONCLUSION

The study conducted an exploratory assessment of the performance of non-referral hospitals in Botswana for the period 2006 to 2008 using the Pabón Lasso technique. The results show that during each year in the period, less than half of the hospitals operated efficiently while more than half operated with excess bed capacity.

The findings of the study imply that instead of expanding hospital sizes by increasing the number of beds, there could be an expansion in the health services provided by these hospitals. This finding also provides an opportunity to improve upon maternal and child health services, which will not only reduce infant, child and maternal deaths and accelerate progress towards the health-related Millennium Development Goal targets, but also ensure that progress is made towards universal coverage of health services.

The Pabón Lasso technique provides a simple way of assessing the performance of health facilities using routine data from health facilities. The Ministry of Health of Botswana needs to consider applying this technique to annual data collected from hospitals in the country as part of institutionalizing efficiency monitoring within the health management information systems framework.

Inspite of the importance of this study in highlighting the issues of inefficiency in non-referral hospitals in Botswana with the use of the Pabón Lasso technique, it is important to note that conclusions from the study findings might not apply to other categories of health facilities other than those sampled for the study.

ACKNOWLEDGMENTS

The authors are grateful to WHO Country Office in Botswana for facilitation; Ministry of Health, Botswana for authorization and the various hospitals for participating in the study. We also acknowledge the role played by University of Botswana in serving as host and participants of the dissemination workshops. The field work was funded by WHO Regional Office for Africa.

The views expressed in this article are those of the authors only and does not represent the views of WHO, University of Botswana, University of Ghana or any other Organization mentioned.

CONTRIBUTIONS OF AUTHORS

Data was collected by JN and NT. JN, NT, LGS, EAN, EZA and JMK contributed to the design, analysis and writing of various sections of the chapter. All authors read and approved the final chapter.

REFERENCES

[1] World Health Organization. World Health Statistics 2009. Report. Geneva: World Health Organization2009 2009. Report No.: 97892-4-156381-9.

[2] World Health Organization. The world health report: health systems financing: the path to universal coverage. Geneva: World Health Organization2010.

[3] Tlotlego, N; Nonvignon, J; Sambo, LG; Asbu, EZ and Kirigia, JM. Assessment of productivity of hospitals in Botswana: a DEA application. *Int. Arch. Med.* 2010 2010/11/09;3:27.

[4] Kirigia, JM; Fox-Rushby, J and Mills, A. A cost analysis of Kilifi and Malindi district hospitals in Kenya. *African Journal of Health Sciences.* 1998;5:79-84.

[5] Emrouznejad, A; Parker, B and Tavares, G. Evaluation of research in efficiency and productivity: A survey and analysis of the first 30 years of scholarly literature in DEA. *Socio-Economic Planning Sciences.* 2008;42:151-7.

[6] O'Neil, L; Rauner, M; Heidenberger, K and Kraus, M. A cross-national comparison and taxonomy of DEA-based hospital efficiency studies. *Socio-Economic Planning Sciences.* 2008;42:158-89.

[7] Kirigia, JM; Emrouznejad, A; Sambo, LG; Munguti, N and Liambila, W. Using Data Envelope Analysis to Measure Technical Efficiency of Public Health Centres in Kenya. *Journal of Medical Systems* 2004;38(2):155-66.

[8] Osei, D; d'Almeida, S; George, MO; Kirigia, JM; Mensah, AO and Kainyu, LH. Technical efficiency of public district hospitals and health centres in Ghana: a pilot study. *Cost-effectiveness and Resource Allocation.* 2005;39.

[9] Nakamba, P; Hanson, K and McPake, B. Markets for hospital services in Zambia. Int J Health Plann Manage [serial on the Internet]. 2002; 17.

[10] Walker, D and Mohammed, RL. Producing health services efficiently: a review of measurement tools and empirical applications: Oxford Policy Institute2004.

[11] UNDP. Human Development Report 2010. New York: Palgrave Macmillan; 2010.

[12] World Bank. World Development Indicators database2010: Available from: http://data.worldbank.org/data-catalogue.

[13] UNDP. Human Development Report 2009. Oxford: Oxford University Press; 2009.

[14] Central Statistics Office. Stats briefs. Gaborone: Central Statistics Office,2009.

[15] Barnum H and Kutzin, J. Public hospitals in developing countries: resource use, cost, financing. Baltimore: Johns Hopkins University Press; 1993.

[16] Malawi MOH/WHO. Technical efficiency of district hospitals in Malawi: an exploratory analysis using data envelopment analysis. 2008.

[17] Pabón Lasso, H. Evaluating hospitals performance through simultaneous application of several indicators. *Bull of the Pan American Health Organ*. 1986;20:341-57.

[18] UK Department of Health. Hospital organisation, specialty mix and MRSA2007 Contract No.: 9163.

In: Health Insurance
Editors: E. Abrahamsen et al.

ISBN: 978-1-62081-050-7
© 2012 Nova Science Publishers, Inc.

Chapter 4

PUBLIC LONG-TERM CARE INSURANCE SYSTEM IN JAPAN

Masakazu Washio[*,a,b], *Yumiko Arai*[c],
Asae Oura[b] *and Mitsuru Mori*[b]

[a]Department of Community Health and Clinical Epidemiology,
St. Mary's College, Fukuoka, Japan
[b]Department of Public Health,
Sapporo Medical University School of Medicine, Hokkaido, Japan
[c]Department of Gerontology Policy (Health for Aged),
National Institute of Longevity Sciences, Morioka-cho, Aichi, Japan

ABSTRACT

Improvements in public health and advances in medicine after World War II have given Japan one of the highest life expectancies in the world. The dramatic increase in the number of older people in this country is well documented. Because the birth rate dropped sharply after the postwar baby boom, population aging is proceeding more rapidly than in any other industrialized nation. Due to the increased population, the number of elderly in need of care has also increased.

---

[*] Tel: +81- 942- 35 -7582, Fax: +81- 942- 34- 9125 E-mail: washio@st-mary.ac.jp

It is estimated that the number of elderly in need of care will reach 5.2 million in 2020. Therefore, in April 2000, a new public long-term care insurance system (LTCIS) was launched in Japan, making it the third country to do so, after the Netherlands and Germany.

Although Japanese LTCIS follows the German LTCIS, there are some differences between the two countries. First, the elderly in need of care and their caregivers choose to receive care services or cash payment for family-based caregiving in German, while only care services are available in Japan. Second, caremanager, who arranged care services as well as assess the effect of care services, help users to make a care plan in Japan, although the idea of care management was adopted from the United Kingdoms' system. In this chapter, we introduce Japanese LTCIS and our studies on the care burden among caregivers before and after the introduction of this system.

1. INTRODUCTION

Improvements in public health and advances in medicine after World War II have given Japan the one of the highest life expectancies in the world, i.e., 79.0 years for men and 85.8 years for women in 2006[1]. On the other hand, live birth rate (per 1,000 Japanese population) decreased from 34.3 in 1947 to 9.5 in 1997[2]. Because the birth rate dropped sharply after the postwar baby boom, population aging is proceeding more rapidly than any other industrialized nation [3]. The dramatic increase in the number of older people in Japan, which is now well documented [3], has led to a concurrent increase in the number of the frail elderly (i.e., the elderly who need care) [4, 5]. It is estimated that the number of the frail elderly will reach 5.2 million in 2020[6]. Family caregivers are often both physically and mentally burdened with caring for their frail elderly [6].

In former days, the frail elderly were cared for by the traditional family system because most Japanese elderly, over 60% compared with 20% or less in the Western countries, lived with their children [3]. However, the number of children in each family has dramatically decreased, and the nuclear family has become more common (i.e., 59.0% in 2006)[1, 2, 7]. Therefore, caregivers often have to care for the frail elderly without help from other relatives because they often live too far away to provide assistance. Several reports [8, 9] demonstrated that a large amount of time spent on caregiving was related to the feeling among such caregivers of carrying an insupportable burden. It has been reported that caring for the elderly may induce depression in the caregivers [10]. Caregiver's depression is an important social problem in Japan because it involved the potential risk of caregivers discontinuing caregiving at home [11].

In Japan, the environment for the elderly and their caregivers has undergone momentous changes. In April 2000, to promote greater autonomy of the frail elderly in daily life as well as to reduce burden on their caregivers, the public long-term care insurance system for the elderly (LTCIS) was launched in Japan, making it the third country, after the Netherlands [12] and Germany [13], provide such insurance. The fundamental purpose of LTCIS is the establishment of what can be called 'universalism' in elderly care policy [14]. First, under the new public LTCIS, all of the frail elderly in Japan can use elderly care services according to their degree of need of care, while the elderly care services in Japan were formerly reserved for users from low income households before LTCIS was implemented (i.e., under the old selective tax scheme). Second, the users themselves can determine their individual need for services under LTCIS, while the administration of service was determined by public administrative agencies before LTCIS. Third, LTCIS allows both profit-based and non-profit private organizations to provide elderly care services, while the service providers were confined to municipal governments and non-profit private organizations stipulated by the Social Welfare Law before LTCIS. Fourth, the insurers are required to bear the co-payment depending on the service utilized under LTCIS, while the elderly paid only limited fees before LTCIS. Last, the middle aged (40-64 years old) are also required to become members of LTCIS in order to assist in bearing the cost of this insurance system because their parents may use services under LTCIS.

Although Japanese LTCIS follows the German LTCIS, there are some differences between the two countries concerning this insurance system. First, the frail elderly and their caregivers can choose to receive either care services or a cash payment for family-based caregiving in Germany, while only care services are available in Japan [15]. Second, caremangers, who arrange care services as well as assess the effect of care services, help users to make care plan in Japan [16], although the idea of care management [17] was adopted from the United Kingdoms' system.

In a rural town in Kyushu, the southernmost of the four main islands of Japan, study on the burden of family caregivers of the frail elderly with home-visiting nursing service was conducted in 1998[18], 2 years before the introduction of this insurance system in Japan. In these studies, a Japanese version of the Center for Epidemiologic Studies Depression Scale (CES-D)

[19, 20] and a Japanese version of the Zarit caregiver Burden Interview (ZBI) [21, 22, 23] were used to evaluate the depressive state and burden of family caregivers. In this paper, we introduce our studies on the Japanese elderly and their family caregivers in this town before and after the introduction of this system [18, 24]. We also introduce other studies on the Japanese elderly and their family caregivers conducted in other area [25, 26, 27, 28, 29, 30, 31, 32].

2. DEPRESSION AMONG CAREGIVERS OF THE FRAIL ELDERLY IN A RURAL TOWN IN SOUTHERN JAPAN BEFORE AND AFTER THE PUBLIC LONG TERM CARE INSURANCE SYSTEM FOR THE ELDERLY

In a rural town in Kyushu, the southernmost of the four main islands of Japan, studies on the burden of family caregivers of the frail elderly with home-visiting nursing service started in 1998, 2 years before the introduction of this insurance system in Japan. We would like to show the results of cross sectional study from 1998 to 2004 [24].

Table 1 shows the trends in the depressive rate of family caregivers and other characteristics of the family caregivers, 1998-2004. In a rural town with only one home-visiting nursing service station, the depressive rate among caregivers was 56.3% before LTCIS.

After the introduction of LTCIS, the rate decreased to 47.5% in the fifth year but the difference did not reach significant level. With the decreased depressive rate of caregivers, ZBI decreased from 41.9 ±20.7 (mean±SD) to 35.0 ±19.5. On the other hand, the proportion of either male caregivers, old caregivers with the age of 65 years and over, spouse caregivers, or caregivers who consulted with doctors for their own medical conditions did differ before and after LTCIS.

Table 2 illustrates the trends in the characteristics of the frail elderly with home-visiting nursing service, 1998-2004. Compared with before LTCIS, age of the frail elderly and the proportion of the old elderly with the age of 80 years and over significantly increased at the first of LTCIS but decreased at the third year and the fifth year of LTCIS. The proportion of bedridden elderly was 75.0% before the LTCIS while the rate decreased to 55.0% at the fifth years of LTCIS.

Table 1. The trends in the depressive rate of family caregivers and other characteristics of the family caregivers in a rural town in southern Japan before and after the public long term care insurance for the elderly (LTCIS), 1998-2004. (Washio et al. 2005)[24]

Characteristics Of caregivers	Before LTCIS 1998 (n=48)	1st year of LTCIS 2000 (n=50)	3rd year of LTCIS 2002 (n=50)	5th year of LTCIS 2004 (n=40)
Depressive rate	27(56.3)	28(56.0)	22(44.0)	19(47.5)
CES-D	17.5 ±9.6	18.9 ±11.2	17.1 ±9.7	17.4 ±10.2
ZBI	41.9 ±20.7	41.5 ±18.6	33.9 ±17.2	35.0 ±19.5
Males	10(20.8)	10(20.0)	11(22.0)	14(35.0)
Age	60.4 ±14.3	64.4 ±12.2	64.2 ±11.2	65.5 ±11.6
65 years old	20(41.7)	24(48.0)	24(48.0)	22(55.0)
and over	20(41.7)	23(46.0)	25(50.0)	21(52.5)
Spouses	33(68.8)	39(78.0)	29(58.0)	26(65.0)
Consulted with own doctors				

Values are expressed as number(%) or mean ± SD.
CES D: the Center for Epidemiologic Studies Depression Scale
ZBI: the Zarit caregiver Burden Interview

In contrast, the rates of demented elderly were around 50% during the study periods. These findings suggest that the frail elderly with high degree of need of care may be institutionalized under the LTCIS.

Table 2. The trends in the characteristics of the frail elderly with home-visiting nursing service in a rural town in southern Japan before and after the public long term care insurance for the elderly (LTCIS), 1998-2004. (Washio et al. 2005) [24]

Characteristics of the frail elderly	Before LTCIS 1998 (n=48)	1st year of LTCIS 2000 (n=50)	3rd year of LTCIS 2002 (n=50)	5th year of LTCIS 2004 (n=40)
Males	23(47.9)	20(40.0)	21(42.0)	16(40.0)
Age	75.7 ±15.6	82.0 ±10.8*	80.2 ±9.3	80.5 ±9.7
80 years old and	20(41.7)	32(64.0)*	28(56.0)	19(47.5)
over Bedridden	36(75.0)	38(76.0)	37(74.0)	22(55.0)*
elderly Dementia	20(41.7)	26(52.0)	26(52.0)	18(45.0)

Values are expressed as number(%) or mean ± SD.
*: p<0.05, vs. before LTCIS (1998)

Table 3. The trends in the care setting and the care service use of the frail elderly with home-visiting nursing service in a rural town in southern Japan before and after the public long term care insurance for the elderly (LTCIS), 1998-2004. (Washio et al. 2005) [24]

Characteristics of the frail elderly	Before LTCIS 1998 (n=48)	1st year of LTCIS 2000 (n=50)	3rd year of LTCIS 2002 (n=50)	5th year of LTCIS 2004 (n=40)
Time spent on caregiving	11.5 ±8.5	15.4 ±8.2*	11.9±8.6	11.8±7.9
(hours/day)	73.6 ±69.4	76.6 ±65.4	78.4 ±89.0	94.5 ±69.1
Duration of caregiving	21(43.8)	24(48.0)	21(42.0)	14(35.0)
(months)	43(89.6)	30(60.0)*	33(66.0)*	38(95.0)
Family members helped with	22(45.8)	34(68.0)*	27(54.0)	20(50.0)
caregiving	24(50.0)	20(40.0)	14(28.0)*	9(22.5)*
Able to go out without	10(20.8)	14(28.0)	16(32.0)	6(15.0)
accompanying the elderly				
Home helper				
Day care/ day service				
Short stay				

Values are expressed as number (%) or mean ± SD.

*: p<0.05, vs. before LTCIS (1998).

Table 3 shows the trends in the care setting and the care service use of the frail elderly. Time on caregiving increased in the 1st year of the LTCIS, but decreased in the 3rd and the 5th year of LTCIS. The rate of caregivers who were able to go out without accompanying the elderly decreased in the 1st and the 3rd year of LTCIS, but increased in the 5th year of LTCIS. The users of home helper increased in the 1st year of LTCIS while the users of day care/day service decreased in the 3rd and the 5th year of LTCIS.

3. RISK FACTORS FOR DEPRESSION AMONG CAREGIVERS OF THE FRAIL ELDERLY IN SOUTHERN JAPAN BEFORE AND AFTER THE PUBLIC LONG TERM CARE INSURANCE SYSTEM FOR THE ELDERLY

Family caregivers are often both physically and mentally burdened with caring for their frail elderly [6]. A cross sectional study was conducted in order to evaluate the factors relating to depression among caregivers of the frail elderly with home-visiting nursing service before and after LTCIS, in 5 towns in Kyushu, the southernmost of the four main islands of Japan [25].

We analyzed 187 pairs of the frail elderly and their caregivers before LTCIS and 155 pairs after LTCIS. Before LTCIS, the frail elderly included 77 males and 110 females with a mean age (±SD) of 81.0±8.0 years while caregivers were 28 males and 159 females with a mean age (±SD) of 61.8±11.8 years.

The kinship statuses of caregivers were 15 husbands, 58 wives, 12 sons, 61 daughters, 34 daughters-in-law, and 7 others. After LTCIS, the frail elderly were 71 males, 83 females and 1 unknown with a mean age (±SD) of 80.1±9.3 years while caregivers were 25 males, 130 females and 1 unknown with a mean age (±SD) of 60.9±13.9 years. The kinship statuses of caregivers were 15 husbands, 54 wives, 9 sons, 44 daughters, 26 daughters-in-law, and 7 others.

Table 4. Odds ratio and 95% confidence intervals for depression among caregivers of the frail elderly before and after the public long term care insurance system for the elderly (LTCIS) in Kyushu, southern Japan (Oura et al. 2007)[25]

Factors	Before LTCIS Odds ratio (95% CI)	After LTCIS Odds ratio(95% CI)
Caregivers characteristics		
Spouse	1.38(0.71, 2.66)	2.92(1.42, 6.01)
Consulting with a doctor about their own	2.99(1.60, 5.60)	4.01(1.97, 8.17)
health	5.17(2.71, 9.87)	6.19(2.92, 13.12)
Felt ill	0.72(0.37, 1.40)	0.47(0.22, 1.00)
Had a job		
Frail elderly characteristics	1.69(0.88, 3.25)	2.79(1.35, 5.74)
Gender (male)	2.75(1.44, 5.25)	2.35(1.14, 4.81)
Dementia with behavioral disturbances		
Care setting	2.77(1.36, 5.67)	1.97(0.92, 4.20)
Attending the elderly more than 16 hours/day	0.82(0.42, 1.60)	0.36(0.17, 0.77)
Being able to go out without accompanying the elderly		

Odds ratio: Adjusted caregiver's gender, caregiver's age, district, and life event.

95% CI: 95% confidence interval.

Depression: CES-D=16 and over.

Table 4 shows adjusted odds ratios and their 95% confidence intervals for depression among caregivers of the frail elderly before and after LTCIS. Before LTCIS, depressive caregivers were more likely to consult with doctor about their own health, to be poor in health, to be caring for the frail elderly who had dementia with behavioral disturbances, and to spend more than 16 hours attending the frail elderly.

After the introduction of LTCIS, depressive caregivers were more likely to be a spouse, to consult with doctor about their own health, to be poor in health, to be caring for a frail elderly male, and to be caring for the frail elderly who had dementia with behavioral disturbances.

Depressive caregivers were less likely to go out without accompanying their frail elderly. Caregivers who had a job had a marginally reduced risk of depression while those attended to the frail elderly more than 16 hours per day showed a non-significantly increase in the risk of depression.

Table 5. The Spearman's rank correlation between caregiver's burden, behavioral disturbances, severity of dementia, level of convenience the caregivers experienced in using services, and hours caregivers can be relieved of duties. (Arai et al. 2004)[26]

Factors	Caregiver's burden, ZBI score (40+ vs. -39)	Behavioral disturbances (1+ vs. 0)	Severity of dementia (3-4 vs. 1-2)	Find it convenient to use services (- vs. +)	Hours caregivers Can be relieved (3+ vs. -2)
Caregiver's burden, ZBI score (40+ vs. -39)	1.00	0.39*	0.32*	0.35*	-0.33*
Behavioral disturbances (1+ vs. 0)		1.00	0.13	0.11	0.04
Severity of dementia (3-4 vs. 1-2)			1.00	1.00	-0.29
Find it convenient to use services (─vs. +)				1.00	-0.21
Hours caregivers can be relieved (3+ vs. -2)					1.00

*:p<0.05

4. FACTORS RELATED TO FEELING OF BURDEN AMONG CAREGIVERS OF THE ELDERLY WITH DEMENTIA IN JAPAN UNDER THE PUBLIC LONG TERM CARE INSURANCE SYSTEM FOR THE ELDERLY

Among 51 elderly who received home-visiting nursing service in Honshu, the central island of the four main islands of Japan, the 46 elderly were found to suffer from dementia [26]. These 46 pairs of the elderly and their caregivers were analyzed to evaluate the factors related to feeling of caregiver's burden. As shown table 5, caregiver's burden was correlated with the patients having behavioral disturbances, severity of dementia, level of convenience the caregivers experienced in using services, and hours caregivers can be relieved.

5. FACTORS RELATED TO ADMISSION OR INSTITUTION AMONG THE FRAIL ELDERLY WITH HOME-VISITING NURSING SERVICE IN KYUSHU, SOUTHERN JAPAN

A retrospective follow up study was conducted to evaluate factors associated with admission of the frail elderly to hospitals or nursing homes [27]. In this study, 395 consecutive frail elderly who were receiving domiciliary visits by nurses from a home-visit nursing station in an urban town, in Kyushu, southern Japan between April 1993 and March 1998 (i.e., before LTCIS) were analyzed. The frail elderly were 196 males and 199 females with a mean age ($\pm$SD) of 79.7 $\pm$8.1 years. Table 6 shows risk factors for admission or institution among the frail elderly with home-visiting nursing service before LTCIS. During the six months follow-up, the elderly suffering from malignancy increased the risk of admission while the elderly with severely impaired activities of daily livings reduced the risk. During either one year or two years follow-up, the elderly female and the elderly with severely impaired activities of daily livings were negatively related to admission.

In order to evaluate factors associated with admission of the frail elderly to hospitals or nursing homes, a follow up study was also conducted in Kyushu, southern Japan, from 1998 to 2003 (i.e., from 2 years before LTCIS to the 4th year of LTCIS)[28]. In this study, the participants were 122 pairs of

Table 6. Risk factors for admission or institution among the frail elderly with home-visiting nursing service in an urban town, in Kyushu, southern Japan before the public long term care insurance for the elderly (LTCIS) (Matsuu et al. 2002)[27]

	6 months follow up (n=395) Odds ratio(95% CI)	1 year follow up (n=354) Odds ratio(95% CI)	2 years follow up (n=287) Odds ratio(95% CI)
Social service Number of services used (2+/0-1)	0.85(0.68, 1.07)	1.04(0.83, 1.30)	0.85(0.66, 1.10)
Characteristics of the frail elderly	0.88(0.70, 1.11)	0.89(0.70, 1.12)	0.84(0.64, 1.10)
Age, years old (75+/65-74)	0.82(0.66, 1.02)	0.79(0.63, 0.98)	0.74(0.58, 0.94)
Gender (female/male)	0.99(0.78, 1.27)	1.06(0.83, 1.35)	0.89(0.68, 1.16)
Dementia (yes/no)	1.46(1.09, 1.95)	1.24(0.92, 1.68)	0.88(0.62, 1.26)
Malignancy(yes/no)	0.76(0.60, 0.96)	0.69(0.54, 0.87)	0.69(0.52, 0.91)
Impaired ADL (severe/moderate)			

Odds ratio: adjusted for all factors in the table. 95% CI: 95% confidence interval. ADL: activities of daily livings

frail elderly and their caregivers. The frail elderly were 52 males and 70 females with a mean age (±SD) of 80.7 ±8.5 years at the baseline, while caregivers were 28 males and 94 females with a mean age (±SD) of 61.0 ±13.6 years. The kinship statuses of caregivers were 49 spouses, 51 children, 21 daughters-in-law, and 1 other. The average (±SD) follow-up period was 16.4±1.0 month, ranging from 7 to 30 months.

During the follow-up periods, 16 elderly were admitted to long-term care units while 9 others died at home. These 9 elderly died at home were regarded as successful in-home care and excluded from the analysis because the elderly wanted to stay at home until the end of their life following Japanese tradition. As shown in table 7, frail elderly females were associated with an increased risk of institution while caregivers who were able to go out without accompanying the elderly were associated with a decreased risk.

Table 7. Risk factors for institution among the frail elderly with home-visiting nursing service in Kyushu, southern Japan, from 1998 to 2003 (from 2 years before LTCIS to 4th year of LTCIS) (Oura et al. 2006)[28]

Factors	Hazards ratio (95% confidence interval)
Frail elderly characteristics	
Gender (female/male)	5.33(1.21, 23.45)
Age, years old (80+/-79)	1.58(0.58, 4.36)
Dementia (yes/no)	1.75(0.64, 4.83)
Dementia with behavioral disturbances (yes/no)	2.11(0.76, 5.81)
Caregiver characteristics	
Gender (female/male)	0.64(0.22, 1.85)
Age, years old (65+/-64)	0.79(0.29, 2.18)
Depression (yes/no)	1.32(0.49, 3.56)
Consulted with a doctor about their own health (yes/no)	0.93(0.34, 2.58)
Spouse (yes/no)	0.45(0.15, 1.41)
Daughter-in-law (yes/no)	1.25(0.36, 4.38)
Care setting	
Family member helped with caregiving (yes/no)	0.83(0.30, 2.300)
Being able to go out without accompanying the elderly (yes/no)	0.27(0.10, 0.75)

Depression: CES-D=16 and over.

6. DISCUSSION

Although the rate of depressive caregivers showed non-significant decrease after the introduction of LTCIS, almost half of caregivers were depressive (table 1)[24]. The rate of depression in caregivers is much greater than the rate in general population (1-5%)[33]. More effective support system for caregivers of the frail elderly should be recommended.

As shown in table 3, our study revealed that time spent on caregiving did not decrease after LTCIS[24]. These findings suggest that LTCIS failed to reduce caregiver's burden. Since the degree of mental and/or physical impairment has been considered to a correlate of caregiver's burden[34] and increased utilization of social services has been considered to reduce caregiver's burden[35], the findings of our study may be explained by the following possibility. Under the LTCIS, consumers of nursing/caring service need to pay 10% of price, although they had used such services with no charge before the introduction of this insurance system. In our study [24], the usage of social services decreased under the LTCIS (table 3). They may have reduced utilization of such service. More effective support system for caregivers of the frail elderly should be recommended.

Family caregivers are often both physically and mentally burdened with caring for their frail elderly [6]. A large amount of time spent of time spent on caregiving was reported be a risk factor for heavy burden among caregivers [8, 9]. In our studies, as shown in table 5, attending the elderly more than 16 hours/day was associated with an increased risk of caregiver's depression before LTCIS [25], while caregivers who were able to go out without accompanying the elderly showed an decreased risk of depression before and after LTCIS [25] and under the LTCIS, there was a negative association between caregiver's burden and hours caregivers can be relieved (table 6) [26].

The relationship between the caregiver's burden and behavioral disturbance is well documented [34]. In our studies, dementia with behavioral disturbances increased the risk of depression among caregivers before and after LTCIS (table 5) [25], and there was a positive association between caregiver's burden and behavioral disturbances (table 6) [26].

The level of caregiver's utilization of social services is known to relate to depression [34]. In our study [26], there was a negative association between caregiver's burden and level of convenience for caregivers to use services (table 6) [26]. However, as shown in table 3, the usage of social services decreased under the LTCIS and time spent on caregiving did not decrease after LTCIS [24].

In 1972, the free medical care program for the elderly started at the national level, and the regular health insurance system raised the coverage ratio to 100% for the elderly patients, paid by Finance Ministry subsidy [3]. Today, however, consumers (the frail elderly) have to pay a 10% nursing/caring service fee under the LTCIS because the coverage ratio is 90% for users [1, 6]. Since financial burden was found to be related to depression among caregivers [29], financial burden may restrain caregivers from using social services. In a study [30], we found that the frail elderly and their caregivers used only 30% of services that they had the right to use. Care managers and municipal public health nurses should help them to use municipal services or informal services provided by volunteers.

In our studies, several factors were found as risk factors for institutionalization. Before LTCIS, the elderly with severely impaired activities of daily livings were negatively related to admission (table 6) [27] although the degree of mental and/or physical impairment has been considered to a correlate of caregiver's burden [30]. This may be explained by the following way. First, caring for the severely disabled elderly may be some way easier for caregivers because they need not watch their charges constantly for fear of accidents (e.g., falling, wandering off, and traffic accidents). Second, caregivers of bedridden elderly may not have to go out with accompanying their charges. We did not obtain the information of care setting in this study [27]. However, in other study [28], caregivers who were able to go out without accompanying the elderly were associated with a decreased risk of the institution (table 7). These finding suggest that caregivers may need more supports to reduce mental burden under the LTCIS.

Under the LTCIS, elderly persons have right to use social services [1, 6]. However, in rural Japan, 42 % of healthy elderly people do not want use social services even if they were to become demented [31]. Furthermore, caregiver's concern deters caregivers from using services [32]. Education not only for the frail elderly and their caregivers but also for the general public should be recommended so that anyone can use social services without feeling humiliated.

CONCLUSION

In order to promote greater autonomy of the frail elderly in daily life as well as to reduce burden on their caregivers, LTCIS was launched in Japan. However, the rate of depressive caregivers as well as time spent on caregiving did not decrease under the LTCIS [24]. Although the elderly and their caregivers have right to use services under the LTCIS, they use only small part of these services.

We should overcome the barriers to use social services. Education for the general public should be recommended so that anyone can use social services without feeling humiliated. In addition, municipal services or informal services provided should be provided when the elderly and their caregivers cannot afford to use social service under the LTCIS.

REFERENCES

Health and Welfare Statistics Association (2007). *Trend of National Health 2007*. Tokyo, Japan: Health and Welfare Statistic Association (in Japanese).

Health and Welfare Statistics Association (1998). *Health and Welfare Statistics in Japan 1998.* Tokyo, Japan: Health and Welfare Statistic Association.

Campbell J.C. (1992). *How policies change: the Japanese Government and the Aging Society.* Princeton, UK: Princeton University Press.

Arai Y. (2001). Japan's new long-term care insurance. *Lancet,* 357: 1713.

Watts J. (1998). Caring for Japan's elderly; mission impossible? *Lancet,* 352:798.

Maeda D. (2003). The outline of new public long-term care insurance program. In F. Takagi (Eds.), *Aging in Japan 2003*, (pp.188-191). Tokyo, Japan: Japan Aging Research Center.

Kono S. (2003). Demographic aspects of population aging in Japan. In F. Takagi (Eds.), *Aging in Japan 2003*, (pp7-51). Tokyo, Japan: Japan Aging Research Center.

Rabins P.V., Fitting M.D., Esatham J., et al. (1990). Emotional adaptation over time in caregivers for chronically ill elderly people. *Age Aging,* 19: 185-190.

Walker A.J., Acock A.C., Bowman S.R., et al. (1996). Amount of caregiven and caregiving satisfaction: a latent growth curve analysis. *J. Gerontol: Psycol Sci*, 51 B: 130-142.

Barnes C.L., Given B.A., Given C.W. (1992). Caregivers of elderly relatives; spouses and adult children. *Health Soc. Work,* 17: 282-289.

Arai Y., Sugiura M., Washio M., et al. (2001). Caregiver depression predicts early discontinuation of care for disabled elderly at home. *Psychiatry Clin .Neurosci.,* 55: 379-382.

Campen C., Gameren E. (2005). Eligibility for long-term care in the Netherlands: development of a decision support system. *Health Soc. Care Community* 13: 287-296.

Tesch-Romer C. (2001). Intergenerational solidarity and caregiving. *Z. Gerontol. Geriatr,* 34: 28-33.

Shimizu Y. (2003). Development of public long term care insurance and future direction of the elderly care. In F. Takagi (Eds.), *Aging in Japan 2003*, (pp 197-204). Tokyo, Japan: Japan Aging Research Center.

Washio M. (1999). Family caregiving and cash payment for family caregiving. *Nihon Iji Shinpo (Jap Med J)*, 3942: 79-80. (in Japanese).

Washio M., Arai Y. (1998). The expected role for care mangers under the public long term care insurance for the elderly. *Nihon Iji Shinpo (Jap Med J)*, 3891: 73-76. (in Japanese).

Scottish office social work services group (1991). *Care management and assessment, practitioner's guide.* London, UK: HMSO Publication Centre.

Washio M., Arai Y. (1999). Depression among caregivers of the disabled elderly in southern Japan. *Psychiatry Clin. Neurosci.,* 53: 407-412.

Radloff L. (1977). The CES-D scale: a self reported depression scale for research in the general population. *Appl. Psychol. Measurement,* 1: 385-401.

Shima S., Shikano T., Kitamura T., et al. (1985). Reliability and validity of CES-D. *Seishin Ikagu (Jpn. J. Psychiatry),* 27: 717-723 (in Japanese).

Zarit S.H., Reaver K.E., Bach-Peterson J. (1980). Relatives of the impaired elderly: Correlates of feelings of burden. *Gerontologist,* 20: 649-655.

Zarit S.H., Tood P.A., Zarit J.M. (1986). Subjective burden of husband and wives as caregivers. *Gerontologist,* 26: 260-265.

Arai Y., Kudo K., Hosokawa T., et al. (1997). *Psychiatry Clin Neurosci,* 51: 281-287.

Washio M., Arai Y., Oura A., et al. (2005). Careburden and depression among caregivers of the frail elderly with home-visiting nursing service before and after the introduction of the public long term care insurance for the elderly: the findings from the studies until the fifth year of the insurance system. *Rinsho to Kenkyu,* 82: 1366-1370. (in Japanese).

Oura A., Washio M., Arai Y., et al. (2007). Depression among caregivers of the frail elderly in Japan before and after the introduction of the public long-term care insurance system. *Z. Gerontol. Geriatr.,* 40: 112-118.

Arai Y., Kumamoto K., Washio M., et al. (2004). Factors related to feelings of burden among caregivers looking after impaired elderly in Japan under the long-term care insurance system. *Psychiatry Clin. Neurosci.,* 58: 396-402.

Matsuu K., Washio M., Arai Y., et al. (2002). Factors related to admission or institution among the frail elderly with a home-visiting nursing service. *Nihon Koshu Eisei Zasshi (Jpn J Public Health),* 49, 1107-1116 (in Japanese).

[28] Oura A., Washio M., Wada J, et al. (2005). Factors related to institutionalization among the frail elderly with home-visiting nursing service in Japan. *Gerontology,* 52: 66-68.

Washio M., Inoue H., Kiyohara C., et al. (2003). Depression among caregivers of patients with chronic obstructive pulmonary disease. *Intern. Med. J.,* 10: 255-259.

Washio M., Yoshida H., Saitoh S., et al. (2004). Risk factors for heavy burden among family caregivers. *Koureisha Mondai Kennkyu (Research on the issues of the elderly),* 20: 1-4. (in Japanese).

Arai Y., Kudo K., Washio M. (1998). Caring for Japan's elderly. *Lancet,* 352 (9137): 1393.

Arai Y., Sugiura M., Miura H., et al. (2000). *Int. J. Geriatr Psychiatry,* 15: 961-968.

Arai Y. (2007). Present status and trends of mental disorders. In S. Suzuki, S hisamichi (Eds.), *Simple Hygiene and Public Health 2007,* (pp.299-303). Tokyo, Japan: Nanzando. (in Japanese).

Baumgarten M.(1989). The health of persons giving care to the demented elderly: a critical review of the literature. *J. Clin. Epidemiol.,* 42: 1137-1148.

Bass D.M., Noelder L.S., Rechlin L.R. (1996). The moderating influence of service use on negative caregiving consequences. *J. Gerontol.,* 51 B: 121-131.

In: Health Insurance
Editors: E. Abrahamsen et al.

ISBN: 978-1-62081-050-7
© 2012 Nova Science Publishers, Inc.

Chapter 5

INTEGRATION OF HEALTH INSURANCE AND CARE PROVISION: DOES IT IMPROVE SERVICE DELIVERY?

Arthur Hayen[*]*, Bert R Meijboom and Gert P Westert*
Faculty of Social and Behavioral Sciences, Tilburg University,
Tilburg, the Netherlands

ABSTRACT

What happens to the delivery of health services when health insurers integrate with care providers? Health insurers and care providers can choose among different methods when organizing their mutual transactions. We distinguish between standard market- and hierarchical organization. In hierarchies, health insurance and care provision are integrated and coordinated by an overarching entity. This entity may want to lower costs in order to increase its profits. While this behavior may be desirable in light of the growing costs of health care, consumers and policy-makers fear that this containment of costs will come at the expense of quality. We test both hypotheses by analyzing empirical literature and find a strong negative link between integration and costs. Regarding quality, evidence is mixed. Integration seems to alter care experiences, reflecting skepticism towards or discomfort with the entity's dominant

---

[*] Correspondence: Arthur Hayen, MSc, PhD student, Tilburg University, Faculty of Social Sciences, Tranzo, POBox 90153, 5000 LE Tilburg, the Netherlands. Tel: +31 13 466 8271; E-mail: A.P.Hayen@uvt.nl.

role in providing health care. Objective quality data, such as mortality rates, fail to show a consistent negative effect of integration on health. Regarding the effect of integration on care processes, hierarchies excel in the provision of preventive care, but underprovide services to those who are most in need of health care. We explain our findings by referring to incentive structures at both the organizational and physician level. We conclude that integration of health insurance and care provision may only be beneficial for subgroups of patients. This implies that, optimally, governments should create a legal base for hierarchical organization while initiating quality transparency, such that these subgroups can select themselves into hierarchies.

Keywords*: Transaction cost theory, organization, service delivery.

INTRODUCTION

An extreme form of self-sufficiency in organizing health care would be a single person who masters the medical profession on their own, only to treat themselves when fallen ill. Currently, autarkic organization is rare among developed countries: today's economic landscape is filled with specialists who all have specialized in what they can do most efficiently (1). The possibility to transact with one another is vital for the survival of this specialist economy. Transacting with others is considered a gainful enterprise as it implies that one can stick to the production of a particular commodity, while using the revenues of this production to obtain the remainder of the necessary resources from other specialists. By doing so, talents are exploited and economies of scale are reached.

Exemplary of a specialist economy, health insurance and care are often provided by separate parties. Therefore, both parties need to contract with each other: care providers agree to provide health services to the population of insured, in exchange for part of the insurance premiums. Transacting requires organization, however. Several organizing methods exist through which parties can execute the various tasks that together help the process of transacting (2). These organizing methods differ from each other in the way they coordinate the economic behavior of the involved parties. For example, parties can choose to remain autonomous and thus to be coordinated by market prices and volumes: 'the price system'. Parties may also opt for hierarchical organization, implying that they lose autonomy and are instead coordinated by a single overarching entity: 'hierarchy'. In that case, we say that health insurance and care provision are *integrated*. The distinction between the two is depicted in Figure 1.

With the passage of the Health Insurance Act of 2006, the Dutch government allowed for what we call *hierarchical organization* within dyads of transacting health insurers and care providers. The government linked care providers' autonomy vis-à-vis health insurers to the increasing costs of providing care and reasoned that health insurers should be put in a position to exert a greater influence over the quality and efficiency of care providers. Two legal provisions were made that facilitate health insurers in exerting this influence: all health insurers were allowed to contract selectively with care providers, and to provide care themselves. In part, this change was realized by lifting the distinction between public and private health insurers, as public health insurers used to have a legal duty to contract all care providers in their working area. While it was expected that health insurers, who were now put in a position to compete on the quality and efficiency of the contracted care, would actually do so, this turned out to be a fallacy. Several reasons are given for health insurers' passive stance towards hierarchical organization, amongst which is their fear of losing enrollees (3). After all, as witnessed by the public backlash against HMOs in the US, consumers and patients are skeptical about health insurers meddling with the provision of care by coordinating care providers. In this article we discuss whether there is an empirical base for this skeptical stance towards hierarchical organization within dyads of health insurers and care providers.

The remainder of the paper is organized as follows. First, we develop a theoretical framework around organizing methods, with which we can put research findings into perspective. After that, we analyze several studies that are informative about the effect of integrated health insurance and care provision (henceforth denoted as 'integration') on the quality and costs of care. We end this paper with several implications for practice and ideas for further research.

TRANSACTION COST THEORY AND ITS USE IN PUBLIC POLICY DISCOURSE

Transacting requires the execution of various tasks – and the organization thereof – (2). *First,* both parties to the transaction must collect information so as to be able to make well-reasoned decisions on whom to contract. Information must be collected on both the willingness of potential contract partners to realize gains from transacting and their ability to do so. Amongst others, the ability of contract partners refers to the quality of care they can realize. *Second*, once a possible contract partner has been identified, both parties need to bargain over the terms of the contract. These terms may include a "formula for dividing [the anticipated] gains" (2) and the abilities to which parties lay claim. *A final set of tasks* is aimed at the enforcement of the contractual terms. These tasks are not merely of legal kind. Even though the Williamsonian framework (4) devotes attention to legal instruments such as litigation and arbitration, which should guarantee parties' obedience to the letter and the spirit of the contract, transaction cost theorists seem to pay most attention to reward schemes aimed at aligning the economic interests of the parties involved. Reward schemes align interests by means of (financial) incentives.

The execution of the above mentioned tasks is complicated by both human and environmental factors. Think of bounds on our cognitive abilities constraining our information processing capability, rapidly changing contractual environments, or market conditions that could give way to opportunistic behavior in contract parties (indicative of diverging economic interests). Paying due attention to the presence of these complicating factors, transaction cost theorists are concerned with finding optimal methods through which the above described tasks can be executed. These methods are called 'organizing methods', and differ from each other in the way they coordinate the economic behavior of the parties involved (2). Differences in coordination across organizing methods are reflected in differences in the execution of tasks. For example, within the price system parties are coordinated by market prices and volumes and are rewarded as such. Given market prices, a higher volume implies a higher reward. Hierarchies, on the other hand, reward on the basis of input: one's obedience to the directives advanced by the overarching entity. This reward may take the form of a fixed salary, independent of output by definition. These reward systems are expected to have a differing impact on the behavior of care providers. In case a care provider's reward depends on the output produced, demand may be induced in order to generate higher rewards (income). When receiving a fixed salary care providers may want to minimize effort instead. These differences in expected behavior have proved to be important to policy, to be discussed next.

Today, as well in the past, governments have decided upon whether or not to allow health insurers and care providers to organize their transactions through hierarchy. That is, whether or not to let them integrate. In practice, hierarchical organization implies that care providers give up at least some of their autonomy for the benefit of the health insurer's profits. From a policy point of view, this may or may not be deemed desirable. With the passage of the Health Maintenance Organization (HMO) Act in 1973, US Congress explicitly gave their consent to hierarchical forms of organization within dyads of health insurers and care providers, and even provided financial support to those who resorted to hierarchy. The HMO Act was signed in a time in which rapidly increasing medical costs were placing significant pressure upon government budgets. In the build-up to the Act's development, Ellwood, who was supported by the US Department of Health, Welfare and Education, explained the surging medical costs by referring to the health system's reward structure (5). In the 1970s, fee-for-service arrangements (incorporated into indemnity plans) were the dominant form of health insurance, implying that health insurers and care providers remained autonomous and organized their mutual transactions at arm's length: health insurers were simply supposed to pay the bill, and did not have a say in physician choice or treatment decisions (left part of Figure 1). Ellwood recognized that this autonomy of care providers implied that health insurers could not prevent them from driving up output, both in terms of quantity and resource intensity. This observation led him to suggest that health insurers must be placed in a position to break the connection between output and reimbursement. Early HMOs, 'staff model HMOs', were entities in which the insurance function and care provision function were integrated: all care providers, amongst which were primary care providers, were paid a fixed salary. Hence, at least in theory, the organizational design of staff model HMOs was such that it broke the connection between output and reimbursement. It removed care providers' economic incentive to drive up output beyond what is medically necessary, since they would not get paid for these additional efforts. Apart from paying a fixed salary to their primary care providers, HMOs are distinctive in that they explicitly meddle with the provision of care. For example, access to specialist care is only granted upon one's general practitioner's referral. Furthermore, the general practitioner's actions, including his/her referral policy, are under review by the HMO and bonuses may be awarded based on this utilization review. Besides these policies that appear in the contract of affiliated general practitioners, HMOs may maintain tacit agreements on resource utilization that are enforced by a flexible redundancy policy.

All these are ways in which the HMO, the overarching entity, coordinates the behavior of care providers.

The resulting hierarchical organization is often linked to *lower total cost of care* because of its incentive structure(s). Concerns are voiced over these incentive structures' effect on quality however, since, from an economic perspective, physicians may be inclined to exert less effort when pay is independent of output. Besides, the overarching entity itself may initiate cost-savings initiatives, *possibly compromising on quality*. Traditional indemnity plans and HMOs, so to speak, occupy opposite ends on a price system – hierarchy continuum. Several intermediate institutional forms have emerged over the years, which combine elements of both the price system and hierarchy. In the US, we have witnessed the rise of Preferred Provider Organizations (PPO), Point-of-Service plans (POS) and several network HMOs (IPA). To determine the position these institutions occupy on a price system – hierarchy continuum, we pay attention to whether an overarching entity is present to coordinate the behavior of health insurers and care providers, and whether the parties to the transaction are rewarded for input. As both are characteristic of hierarchical organization, a positive response to either one or both questions implies that the particular institution moves to the right of the price system – hierarchy continuum. Relying on several rich accounts of these institutions, we have drawn the following continuum (see Figure 2).

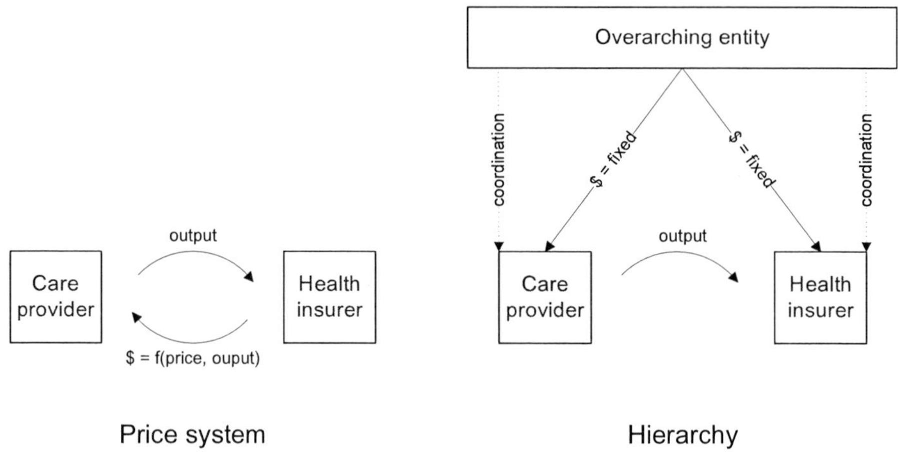

Figure 1. The price system and hierarchy. '$' refers to 'income'.

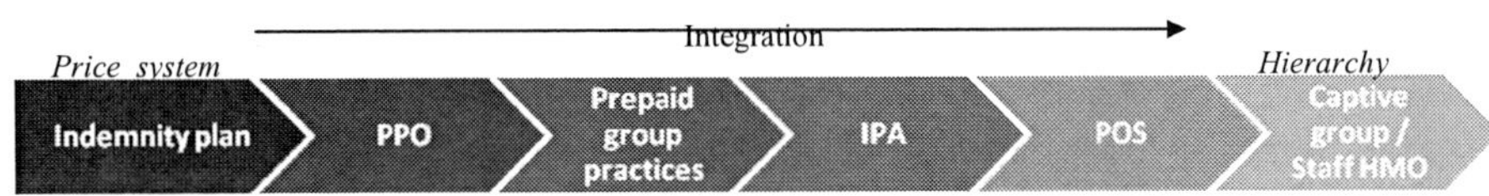

Figure 2. The price system – hierarchy continuum, containing institutions that use (a mix of) the price system and hierarchy. When institutions move to the right, health insurance and care provision become more integrated.

In the remainder of this paper, we investigate whether institutions to the right of this continuum incur lower costs by compromising on quality. As discussed in the above, this effect is associated with integration, both by transaction cost theorists and practitioners.

THE EFFECT OF HEALTH INSURER – CARE PROVIDER INTEGRATION ON QUALITY

Studies on quality differentials across institutions have used a broad variety of quality indicators. Broadly, we can distinguish between subjective/objective outcome indicators and subjective/objective process indicators. Among outcome indicators are self-reported health and satisfaction (subjective) and mortality (objective). Exemplary of process indicators are perceived availability or accessibility (subjective), and measures indicating whether care has been provided according to professional standards or guidelines (objective). In the next sections, we structure our discussion on quality based on this distinction in subjective/objective indicators on the one hand and outcome/process indicators on the other hand.

Subjective Outcome Indicators

The US Medicaid Managed Care (MMC) program was called into existence to control Medicaid spending at the State level. This program substitutes hierarchically organized HMO plans for traditional fee-for-service plans. The participating HMOs were paid a capitation fee in advance. A capitation fee is a fixed amount per enrollee, implying that the HMO assumes risk for costs in excess of the capitation fee. This payment structure makes HMOs want to restrain the use of resources by their physicians even more, which could possibly increase their tendency to compromise on quality. The impact the MMC program had on the quality of (primary) care provided to children has been evaluated, by matching recipients of MMC care with a control group receiving care from traditional plans (6). Parents were asked their judgment about the care provided, doctors' "friendliness and courtesy" and their ability to explain things well (6). The authors find that the parents in both groups were equally satisfied with the care provided by the physicians. One reason for why no significant differences across groups are found could be that different kinds of HMOs were grouped together, ranging from more to less integrated. Another study adopted a different approach by clearly distinguishing between indemnity plans, PPOs, POSs and a group including staff HMOs. Similar to our exercise in Figure 2, the authors draw a continuum containing these four institutions. While the theoretical underpinnings of their continuum are somewhat different from ours, we can use transaction cost theory to interpret the results: people are less satisfied with the care provided the more care provision and health insurance are integrated. The respondents' satisfaction with their primary care physician was decreasing with the level of integration, although only the difference between the two extremes on the continuum was significant at the 95% level (7). A further study went into greater depth by subdividing the sample of respondents into those who reported to be healthy and those who reported to be sick. They find that differences in satisfaction across institutions were larger among the sick, who were even less satisfied with forms of integration (8).

Using self-reported health as a subjective outcome indicator, another study found a similar result (9). They studied a population of people who recently had been diagnosed with hypertension, non-insulin-dependent diabetes mellitus, depressive disorder, congestive heart failure or acute myocardial infarction. At the beginning of the study, all respondents were asked to self-report health, which yielded the baseline health against which later responses were compared. Over time, indemnity plans seemed to perform better when compared to hierarchically organized plans. The differences across plans were most pronounced for the vulnerable subpopulations: highly significant drops in self-reported health were found for subpopulations of the elderly and poor individuals with low baseline health.

Both findings can possibly be explained by reward structures at both the organizational and physician level: regarding the former, HMOs that participate in the private for-profit Medicare Advantage plans (8) receive capitation fees from Medicare. These capitation fees have been relatively generous, so as to attract lots of private health insurers (10). Thus, it paid for HMOs to lure large groups of relatively healthy people into their plans as these people are less likely to consume the entire capitation fee. As a result, the generous Medicare fees were employed to design benefit packages targeted at the young and healthy; high-cost beneficiaries, amongst which were the elderly and those in poor health, still had to pay large amounts out-of-pocket (10). At the physician level, receiving a fixed salary is often linked to a reduction in effort, for output is not rewarded. In economics, this reduction in effort is called 'shirking' (2). An HMO's policy to underprovide services in order to save money is called 'stinting' (11). As both behaviors have particularly severe consequences for the ill, levels of satisfaction might be lower in this group.

Objective Outcome Indicators

It is striking to see that although we find strong statistically significant differences in subjective outcomes, favoring price system-based institutions, This trend is not confirmed when analyzing *objective* outcome indicators. Objective outcome indicators have been collected for both acute and chronic diseases. A study investigating acute myocardial infarctions, argues that outcomes might not differ that much for acute diseases (12).

The results of another study (13) indeed suggest this is the case: the authors analyze a national sample of elderly diagnosed with acute myocardial infarction and find no statistically significant difference across institutions in terms of 30-day and 180-day mortality rate. This may reflect the fact that inadequate care, caused by stinting or shirking can lead to immediate death (or other adverse events) in cases of acute illness and is therefore easily detected. Findings are mixed when we investigate populations that require care over a longer period of time, however: other authors study a population of patients diagnosed with colorectal cancer and find no differences in mortality (14), whereas in case of prenatal care, another study found that hierarchy-based institutions perform better (15).

Possibly, this tension between subjective outcomes and objective outcomes can be partially attributed to the public backlash against HMOs, thus reflecting a bias in subjective responses (16). Another explanation could be that care processes differ across institutions, and that these processes affect subjective and objective outcomes differently. In the next subsections we discuss the effect of health insurer – care provider integration on subjective and objective process indicators.

Subjective Process Indicators

The process quality of care can be measured using a wide range of indicators, amongst which are indicators reflecting accessibility, coordination, and the competence of staff. We consider these indicators in turn.

Two studies cited earlier (6,7) asked respondents whether they had experienced unmet or delayed need. These questions directly pertain to the accessibility of both price system and hierarchy-based institutions. In both studies, no significant differences across institutions were found. However, the signs and sizes of the coefficients suggest that when care providers are paid on the basis of outputs, the odds that patients' needs are not (timely) fulfilled are lower when compared to care providers employed by hierarchies. In another study (17) the measure of accessibility was closely related to the one used in the two studies above. This study does find significant differences, however. The surveyed patients were of the opinion that HMOs were significantly less accessible in times of emergency. The results of these studies are in line with what transaction cost theory would predict. After all, physicians' incomes increase with the number of treatments provided, increasing the benefit of being accessible.

HMOs were thought to excel in the coordination of care. This construct was measured by asking patients to rate their physician's awareness of the treatment provided by fellow physicians. Whereas *patients* perceived forms of integrated care to be superior in terms of coordination, responses from a *physician* survey indicate that this may actually not be the case (18). Amongst others, the surveyed physicians indicate to communicate less with physicians to whom patients enrolled in integrated care plans were referred. Furthermore, when referring patients enrolled in integrated care plans, physicians were less inclined to do additional research on specialists with whom they were less familiar. Both are indicative of a lack of coordination in integrated care plans. However, the authors could not control for any response bias due to possible adverse perceptions on integrated care plans.

Another study (19) found that patients of price system-based institutions are significantly more satisfied about both their doctor's level of competence and his/her willingness to discuss problems. Although the latter effect is not interpreted, it could be indicative of the lack of utilization review in price system-based institutions. When such a review system is absent, care providers are not constrained in their efforts to tailor treatment to the specific case at hand (16).

Objective Process Indicators

A further study (20) analyzed a population of individuals diagnosed with depression or schizophrenia. In general, they find higher levels of compliance with professional guidelines in price system-based institutions. However, the authors show that it is actually more costly to comply with professional guidelines, while compliance is not related to symptom reduction. Therefore, one may wonder whether this noncompliance observed in hierarchy-based institutions should be considered bad for these individuals. Another study (13) found for their sample of elderly diagnosed with acute myocardial infarction, that price system-based institutions have far worse compliance rates with guidelines on the use of intensive care and telemonitoring and the recording of medical histories. They report better compliance rates for the use of diagnostic tests and procedures, but this result does not change their final conclusion that compliance with professional guidelines is lower in price system-based institutions. Another study (21) examined 1,590 outpatient records of those individuals who recently joined Medicare and for whom new patient evaluations had to be performed. Those in managed care were more likely to have received a wide range of (guideline-recommended) preventive services and check-ups.

No general conclusion regarding guideline compliance can be drawn, as guideline compliance can have several implications. In some cases, complying with evidence-based practice may be cost-efficient whereas in other cases it is not. Therefore, it is difficult to determine ex ante whether guideline compliance is indicative of overuse or whether noncompliance reflects organizational stinting or physicians' shirking.

The study cited in this section (21) is among the many studies that find that HMOs' compliance rates with prevention guidelines are higher. We go into depth on prevention in the next section.

The Effect of Health Insurer – Care Provider Integration on Costs

Several literature reviews on HMO plan performance conclude that these 'extreme' forms of what we have called hierarchical organization are better able to contain cost than their price system-based counterparts (22,23). Multiple reasons exist for why integration between health insurance and care provision could potentially affect the costs of providing care to a population of insured. In the above, we have already mentioned organizational stinting and physicians' shirking, both implying that less care is provided, leading to lower total costs of care. Besides these explanations, the overarching entity coordinating the provision of both health insurance and care is incentivized to be cost-efficient. We therefore observe that coordinated care providers substitute less costly health services or treatments for expensive ones. For example, the coordinating entity may want its primary care physicians to take care of patients or diagnoses commonly treated in secondary care. In sum, integration could lead to a drop in absolute utilization levels and changes in relative utilization levels, the latter referring to differences in the balance of groups of health services. We consider both possibilities in turn. After that, we discuss several 'rival' hypotheses which, if confirmed, could decrease the usefulness of transaction cost thinking when analyzing dyads of health insurers and care providers.

Stinting, Shirking and Substitution

To investigate whether stinting or shirking occurs in integrated institutions, we need evidence of hierarchies withholding care for their enrollees. Furthermore, to separate stinting or shirking from mere cost-efficient behavior, the withheld care has to be of particular importance to the diagnosis- or treatment process. Several studies have investigated the use of coronary angiography (along with cardiac catheterization) in people diagnosed with unstable angina. Although using these techniques can yield several insights into the functioning of one's heart, medical risks are attached to both the placement of the catheters and the use of contrast dye to detect blockages in the coronary arteries. Therefore, potential benefits must outweigh the risks involved in using these imaging techniques. The medical profession distinguishes between discretionary and non-discretionary angiography. Angiography is considered non-discretionary when used in patients "at high risk for future cardiac events" (24). Several studies on differences in the use of angiography across institutions find that hierarchies are significantly less likely to perform angiography (25). Whereas one study (25) speculates that this does not reflect shirking or stinting, another study (24) shows that hierarchies were significantly less likely to perform non-discretionary angiography. The authors conclude that this finding says something important about hierarchies' willingness to provide adequate treatment in situations involving high risk of poor outcomes – high costs – in the short or long run. After all, upon detection of blockages, the patient may request forms of treatment that are either costly or risky.

Withholding non-discretionary angiography is a clear instance of organizational stinting. However, one group of services is particularly prevalent in hierarchies, as compared to price system-based institutions: services aimed at preventing chronic diseases. New enrollees to hierarchical institutions were found to receive more screening tests, such as mammography and pap smears (21). Both tests, aimed at detecting pre-invasive or pre-cancers respectively, allow for an early diagnosis and possibly cost-efficient treatment of those who require long term care. Note how this cost-efficiency differs for the treatment of cardiac events which are often acute in nature (prevention may be less cost-efficient), as opposed to a cancer's chronic nature. A reason for why preventive tests are somewhat underprovided by price system-based institutions could also be that these outputs are not adequately reimbursed (26). The high prevalence of preventive care in hierarchies suggest that integration of health insurance and care provision lead to an increased emphasis on primary health services. The study cited previously (7) provides evidence of this.

The question remains whether this different balance between primary care and secondary care lies at the bottom of the observed cost savings in HMOs. Common knowledge tells us that providing primary care services in lieu of secondary care services can lead to substantial cost savings. Yet, it is not self-evident that primary care can actually substitute for secondary care. Besides, for this substitution to arise, primary care physicians should be accessible. The effect of primary care physicians' accessibility on total costs of care is two-fold. We may both observe the substitution we are after but also an increase in the absolute utilization levels of both primary and secondary care; improved accessibility implies that physicians can meet a higher demand, part of which is shifted onto secondary care providers by virtue of a gate keeping system. Another study (27) tests these hypotheses and finds that primary care substitutes for specialty medical encounters. The authors do not find an effect of accessibility on inpatient or outpatient cost, and speculate that this effect is moderated by the way primary care physicians are compensated. That is, is the organization critical of resource use and does it provide incentives to lower health care utilization? From the seminal work in a further study (28) we know that these elements of hierarchical organization are vital in lowering total costs of care.

Rival Hypotheses: Plan Generosity, Premiums and Patient Mix

It has been quite common in health economics to explain possible cost differentials across institutions by differences in plan generosity, premiums, and deductible-copayment mix (see e.g. (29)). These factors are believed to drive demand and costs accordingly. Next to that, it is argued in these studies that people self-select into institutions and base their choice on the values of these three factors. As a result, different institutions end up having different populations. These differences across populations of patients are believed to be a driving force behind performance differentials across institutions as well. There may be more to the story, however. In this paper, we have adopted a differing perspective and have instead tried to explain performance differentials by referring to the differences in the way health insurers and care providers organize their mutual transactions.

Nevertheless, it is interesting to examine the validity and strength of these 'rival' hypotheses *within the issue of integration.* Although some of these rival hypotheses do not necessarily rule out the possibility that organization is an explanatory factor as well – plan generosity and premiums operate at a different level – they divert attention away from factors at work in the health insurer – care provider dyad, to factors at work in the health insurer – consumer dyad.

In order to make statements about the (relative) importance of organization, one research strategy would be to *control* for other factors: one could formulate a plan generosity index, while also controlling for billing structure. To our knowledge, no studies have done this. Similarly, one could control for patient mix across institutions by adding covariates that reflect the expected take-up of health services. Examples include age, gender, ethnicity and health status indices. All studies discussed in the above have done so, but only to a limited extent.

Other strategies include holding constant rival factors across institutions (e.g. including HMOs and indemnity plans that do not differ in terms of plan generosity), or investigating the performance of hierarchies that 'have been put at a relative disadvantage'. For example, in (30) the total cost of care of a relatively generous HMO was compared with that of an indemnity plan. The authors found that the total cost of care was lower in the HMO, even though from an economic point of view we would expect its plan generosity to drive up costs. This might suggest that organization plays a relatively important role. However, evidence is mixed: the relatively generous HMOs in (31) incur higher total cost of care.

CONCLUSION

Integration of health insurance and care provision matter for the provision of care in general and primary care in specific. In our discussion of the quality and cost implications of integration, we found that integration has the potential to alter care experiences of patients. While several authors argued that the public backlash against HMOs had affected perceived competence of hierarchically coordinated care providers, the finding that *self-reported health* deteriorates for those most in need of health care suggests that their needs are indeed not met. We have linked reward structures at both the organizational and physician level to this finding. These reward structures are such that it pays for both integrated organizations and physicians to spend fewer resources on providing curative care. However, it is challenging to develop a research design that *objectively* measures whether health outcomes are (indeed) worse in hierarchies: we have evaluated studies that analyze a specific group of patients, e.g. those who have been diagnosed with AMI, and found that the evidence was mixed. Studies that analyze an entire population of enrollees, however, are often unable to indicate whether differences in mortality rates across institutions are due to favorable selection (patient mix) or better care (eg (32), (33)). Therefore, more research is needed in order to determine both whether hierarchical organization affects health outcomes and whether transaction cost theory can be a useful paradigm for practice accordingly.

From the discussion on costs we can derive that hierarchies are successful in reducing total cost of care. Here, transaction cost theory may be a promising paradigm for policy. The empirical evidence reviewed here suggests that different cost- or effort-containment strategies are present within hierarchies: organizational stinting, physicians' shirking and substitution. Notably the latter changes the role of the primary care physician within a national health care system.

National and local governments should be aware of these possible effects when establishing a legal base for hierarchical organization. On the other hand, the current situation in the Netherlands suggests that the presence of a legal base for hierarchical organization does not automatically lead to integration of health insurance and care providers. Nowadays, consumers are critical and demand transparency, implying that health insurers have to justify their choice for hierarchical organization and choice of contract partners. The fact that this is a difficult task to do in the absence of reliable information on the quality of care provided by physicians, may explain the lack of selective contracting and other forms of hierarchical organization within the Netherlands (3).

Besides designing a research design with which one can explicitly test the effect of hierarchical organization on quality and costs, future research should incorporate econometric techniques with which one can eliminate the confounding effect of patient mix on quality and cost outcomes. Besides using control variables we encourage the use of strong instrumental variables to link the variation in the unconfounded part in the variable reflecting organization, to quality and costs. While the problem of patient mix is often formulated as differences in (expected) health status across populations, we should also pay attention to differences in *preferences* when conducting research on satisfaction. Controlling for preferences can help to get a better view of a hierarchies' performance in terms of accessibility, coordination and professional competence. From a policy perspective, controlling for preferences can help to identify subgroups of people for whom hierarchical organization could be beneficial.

After all, we can think of people who want to trade organizational access or professional competence for financial access, especially those who are relatively healthy. Therefore, in an attempt to increase social welfare, governments should allow for a broad variety of institutions reflecting the different needs of consumers and patients. Again, the availability of information on quality and transparency of care processes, are vital for guiding consumers and patients to the institute that employs the optimal level of integration between health insurance and care provision.

REFERENCES

[1]   North DC. Institutions. *J Econ Perspect* 1991;5(1):97-112.

[2]   Hennart JF. Explaining the swollen middle: Why most transactions are a mix of "market" and "hierarchy". *Organ Sci* 1993;4(4):529-47.

[3]   Westert GP, Burgers JS, Verkleij H. The Netherlands: regulated competition behind the dykes? *Brit Med J* 2009;339:839-42.

[4]   Williamson OE. Comparative economic organization: The analysis of discrete structure alternatives. *Adm Sci Q1991*;36(2):269-96

[5]   Strang D, Bradburn EM. Theorizing legitimacy or legitimating theory? Neoliberaldiscourse and HMO policy. In: Campbell J, Pedersen OK,

eds. *The second movement in institutional analysis: neoliberalism in perspective*. Princeton, NJ: Princeton University Press, 2001:129-58

[6]   Long SK, Coughlin, TA. Impacts of Medicaid managed care on children. *Health Serv Res* 2001;36(1):7-23.

[7]   Reschovsky JD, Kemper P, Tu H. Does type of insurance affect health care use and assessments? *Health Serv Res* 2000;35(1):219-37.

[8]   Keenan PS, Elliot MN, Cleary PD, Zaslavsky AM, Landon B. Quality assessments by sick and healthy beneficiaries in traditional medicare and medicare managed care. *Med Care* 2009;47(8):882-8.

[9]   Ware JE, Bayliss MS, Rogers WH, Kosinski M, Tarlov AR. Differences in 4-year health outcomes for elderly and poor, chronically ill patients treated in HMO and fee-for-service systems. *JAMA* 1996;276(13):1039-47.

[10]   Biles B, Dallek G, Nicholas LH. Medicare advantage: dé-jà-vu all over again? *Health Affair* 2004;(W4):586-97.

[11]   Newhouse JP, Buntin MB, Chapman JD. Risk adjustment and medicare: taking a closer look. *Health Affair* 1997;16(5):26-43.

[12]   Cutler DM, McClellan M, Newhouse JP. How does managed care do it? *Rand J Econ* 2000;31(3):526-48.

[13]   Carlisle DM, Siu AL, Keeler EB, McGlynn EA, Kah KL, Rubenstein LV, et al. HMO vs fee-for-service care of older persons with acute myocardial infarction. *Am J Public Health* 1992;82(12):1626-9.

[14]   Vernon SW, Hughes JI, Hecker VM, Jackson GL. Quality of care for colorectal cancer in a fee-for-service and health maintenance organization practice. *Cancer* 1992;69(10):2418-25.

[15]   Oleske DM, Brance ML, Schmidt JB, Ferguson R, Linn ES. A comparison of capitated and fee-for-service Medicaid reimbursement methods on pregnancy outcomes. *Health Serv Res* 1998;33(1):55-73.

[16]   Mechanic D, Schlesinger M. The impact of managed care on patients' trust in medical care and their physicians. *J Am Med Assoc* 1996;275(21):1693-7.

[17]   Safran DG, Tarlov AR, Rogers WH. Primary care performance in fee-for-service and prepaid health care systems. *J Am Med Assoc* 1994;271(20):1579-86.

[18]   Roulidis ZC, Schulman KA. Physician communication in managed care organizations: opinions of primary care physicians. *J Fam Pract* 1994;39(5):446-51.

[19] Rossiter LF, Langwell K, Wan TTH, Rivnyak M. Patient satisfaction among elderly enrollees and disenrollees in medicare health maintenance organizations. *J Am Med Assoc* 1989;262(1):57-63.

[20] Stiles PG, Boothroyd RA, Dhont K, Beiler PF, Green AE. Adherence to practice guidelines, clinical outcomes, and costs among Medicaid enrollees with severe mental illness. *Eval Health Prof* 2009;32(1):69-89.

[21] Retchin SM, Brown B. The quality of ambulatory care in medicare health maintenance organizations. *Am J Public Health* 1990;80(4):411-5.

[22] Miller RH, Luft HS. Managed care plans: characteristics, growth and premium performance. *Annu Rev Public Health* 1994;15:437-59.

[23] Miller RH, Luft HS. HMO plan performance update: an analysis of the literature 1997-2001. *Health Affair* 2002;21(4):63-86.

[24] Sada MJ, French WJ, Carlisle DM, Chandra NC, Gore JM, Rogers WJ. Influence of payor on use of invasive cardiac procedures and patient outcome after myocardial infarction in the United States: participants in the National Registry of Myocardial Infarction. *J Am Coll Cardiol* 1998;31(7):1474-80.

[25] Every NR, Cannon CP, Granger C, Moliterno DJ, Aguirre FV, Tally JD, et al. Influence of insurance type on the use of procedures, medications and hospital outcome in patients with unstable angina: results from the GUARANTEE registry. *J Am Coll Cardiol* 1998;32(2):387-92.

[26] Battista RN, Spritzer WO. Adult cancer prevention in primary care: contrasts among primary care practice settings in Québec. *Am J Public Health* 1983;73?(9):1040-1.

[27] Fortney JC, Steffick DE, Burgress jr. JF, Maciejewski ML, Petersen LA. Are primary care services a substitute or complement for specialist and inpatient? *Health Serv Res* 2005;40(5):1422-1442.

[28] Kralewski JE, Rich EC, Feldman R, Dowd BE, Bernhardt T, Johnson C, et al. *Health Serv Res* 2000;35(3):591-613.

[29] Manning WG, Newhouse JP, Duan N, Keeler E, Leibowitz A. Health insurance and the demand for medical care: evidence from a randomized experiment. *Am Econ Rev* 1987;77(3):251-77.

[30] Goldman W, McCulloch J, Sturm R. Costs and utilization of mental health services before and managed care. *Health Affair* 1998;17(2):40-52

[31] Goldman DP, Hosek SD, Dixon LS, Sloss EM. The effects of benefit design and managed care on health care costs. *J Health Econ* 1995;14(4):401-18.

[32] Riley G, Lubitz J, Rabey E. Enrollee health status under medicare risk contracts: an analysis of mortality rates. *Health Serv Res* 1991;26(2):137-63.

[33] Maciejewski ML, Dowd B, Call KT, Feldman R. Comparing mortality and time until death for medicare HMO and FFS beneficiaries. *Health Serv Res* 2001;35(6):1245-65.

INDEX

D